New EVERY *Morning*

366 DEVOTIONALS

PEARL BUTTON REASOR

Maximilian Press Publishers
Greenbrier Shoppes
517 Kempsville Road, Suite I
Chesapeake, VA 23320
757-482-2273
aomgt@inter-source.org
info@maximilianpressbookpublishers.com

Maximilian Press Publishers and colophon are registered trademarks of
Maximilian Press Publishing Company.

Manufactured in the United States of America

10 09 08 07 06 05 04 03 02 01

ISBN: 978-0-9827717-8-5

Cover photo: Jason Renard

Cover and layout: www.delaney-designs.com

Edited by Maximilian Press Publishers
A Total Publishing System Company

Other books published by the author:

WHEN WINTER COMES -1982

MY CUP RUNNETH OVER -1996

BESIDE STILL WATERS -2005

New
EVERY
Morning

366 DEVOTIONALS

Pearl D. Reasor
Psalm 113:3

Dedication

New Every Morning is dedicated to the many people
that God has brought, and will continue to bring,
across my path in this life.

I am especially grateful to my daughter Mary
Jane Caudill who spent many hours preparing my
manuscript to submit to the publisher.

New EVERY Morning

Because of the Lord's great love we are not consumed,
for his compassions never fail. They are new every
morning; great is your faithfulness.
Lamentations 3:22-23 NIV

My favorite hymn, "Great Is Thy Faithfulness", by Thomas O. Chisholm, brings out the beauty and truth of God's love for us, as recorded in this Scripture.

Someone has said, "Every New Year—and in reality, every new day is an opportunity to start over and do things in a manner pleasing to God."

"My voice shalt thou hear in the morning, O Lord; in the morning will I direct my prayer unto thee, and will look up." (Psalm 5:3) (KJV)

Morning Prayer

Lord, teach me what I need to know
And show me where I need to go.
Put your desires within my heart;
Your thoughts deep in my mind.
As I seek you day by day,
Your peace and joy I'll find.

Preface

The length of our days is seventy years—or eighty, if we have the strength; Psalm 90:10a

Teach us to number our days aright, that we may gain a heart of wisdom. Psalm 90:12

Realizing that life is short, and having passed my 90th Birthday, I often pause to number my days, asking for wisdom and discernment to know how to use the time God has blessed me with.

Time is a gift from God created for man's benefit.

Truly, His mercies are new every morning and I'm depending on His joy as my strength to accomplish His purpose and plan for my life here as I wait for Him.

May you be renewed every morning as you read and meditate on His Word and revere our all-powerful God.

Great is His Faithfulness!

Pearl Button Reasor

The author lives in Virginia Beach, Virginia. She has been an active member of Kempsville Baptist Church for forty-one years. She teaches a Sunday School Class for women. She has five children, five grandchildren and seven great grandchildren, which she considers a special blessing from the Lord.

Other Books
When Winter Comes   1982
My Cup Runneth Over   1996
Beside The Still Waters   2005

"New Every Morning" is dedicated to the many people that God has brought, and will continue to bring across my path in this life.

Thank you, Lord

I am especially grateful to my daughter Mary Jane Caudill who spent many hours preparing my manuscript to submit to the publisher.

Unless otherwise attributed, all poems are by the author.

January

January 1

God's Will

For I know the plans I have for you, declares the Lord,
plans to prosper you and not to harm you, plans to give
you hope and a future.

Jeremiah 29:11 NIV

The best way to begin the New Year is to focus on what God's plan is for your life. You may say, "I have no idea what His plan is." Think on what you just read—His plan is for your good to give you hope for the future. How He works this out in your life depends upon the choices you make. His plan is for you to make the right choices.

How do we learn to make the right choices? God has provided, in His Word, principles and guidelines to help us make the right choices.

"Trust in the Lord with all your heart; and lean not on your own understanding. In all your ways acknowledge him, and he will make your paths straight." (Proverbs 3:5-6 NIV)

Here we have the first step in knowing God's will. A personal commitment to the Lord Jesus Christ is the right choice for God to fulfill His plan for your life.

May your journey with Christ this year bring fulfillment to many of those plans.

January 2

Security

Yet I am always with you; you hold me by my right hand. You guide me with your counsel, and afterward you will take me into glory.

Psalm 73:23-24 NIV

What more could I ask in this life? God's presence and protection gives peace and security. His provisions sustain me day by day. His Word guides and directs in wisdom and understanding.

When God speaks of His "right hand" it symbolizes His power.

"Your right hand, O Lord, was majestic in power. Your right hand, O Lord, shattered the enemy. (Exodus 15:6 NIV)

"The Lord's right hand is lifted high; the Lord's right hand has done might things!" (Psalm 118:16 NIV)

"My own hand laid the foundations of the earth, and my right hand spread out the heavens; when I summons them they all stand up together." (Isaiah 48:13 NIV)

How great are your promises, O Lord, and your faithfulness has been established.

January 3

God's Word

*My eyes stay open through the watches of the night; that
I may meditate on your promises.*
Psalm 119:148 NIV

Meditation is a discipline that is seldom practiced today. There are too many distractions that claim our attention. As Christians, we need to realize that focusing our mind and spirit on the Lord is critically important in the believer's life. These are the moments that sustain us and stabilize us in our daily life. God's plan for facing troubles is spending time, meditating on His sufficiency and His good, pleasing and perfect will.

Think of 7 P's that will prepare you for problems:

> His presence
> His provisions
> His power
> His protection
> His promises
> His purpose
> His peace

My main resource for meditation is the Word of God where He reveals His character. As I meditate on His ways and practice praise, He gives peace and power to overcome my difficulties. God is our great burden-bearer!

January 4

Waiting on God

*In the morning, O Lord, you hear my voice; in the
morning I lay my request before you and wait in
expectation.*
Psalm 5:3 NIV

The secret of a close relationship with God is to meet Him in the morning. My mind is refreshed, my body is rested and my spirit is rejoicing to see a new day. I can commit the whole day to God, asking for an awareness of His presence and working in my life throughout the day. I'm more aware of my need to wait on Him as I expect Him to solve problems, and direct my thoughts as I make decisions and choices.

Since my choices affect others, as well as myself, it is vital that I wait on the Lord for direction. He is a patient God and His timing is always best. He sometimes uses delays to deepen our trust in Him.

When I feel overwhelmed by a problem, feeling sorry for myself will increase feelings of hopelessness; but crying out to God will turn my attention to the only one who can help.

Attitude of trust—God is good; His plan is worth waiting for.

Attitude of expectancy—He always keeps His Word.

Be still—His timing is always best.

"Blessed is the man who listens to me, watching daily at my doors, waiting at my doorway." (Proverbs 8:34 NIV)

January 5

God is Good

I remember the days of long ago; I meditate on all your works and consider what your hands have done.
Psalm 143:5 NIV

When tempted to be discouraged or depressed take time to think of God and His awesome works. Meditate on His promises and times, in the past, when He has intervened in situations to bring about good in your life.

"You are the God who performs miracles; you display your power among the people." Psalm 77:14

Satan delights in using times of loneliness and weakness, in our lives, to make us feel hopeless. Resist him and cry out with David:

"O Lord, hear my prayer, listen to my cry for mercy; in your faithfulness and righteousness come to my relief." (v. 1) (NIV)

Jesus, My Savior is Lord of my life;
Present to guide me each day.
He stirs my heart with joy and encouragement,
To faithfully seek His will and way.

January 6

Life in Christ

I am the vine; you are the branches. If a man remains
in me and I in him, he will bear much fruit; apart from
me you can do nothing.
John 15:5 NIV

What is your concept of the Christian life? Many church-goers think, "I do my job down here, the Lord does His job up there and someday we'll come together." The idea is that the Christian life is simply something believers "do" and that God, way up in Heaven, hears our prayers and rescues us when we get in trouble.

I confess there was a time in my life when I felt this way. I assumed that in order to be a good Christian I had to do more and work harder for the Lord. I did not take time to nurture my relationship with Christ.

Then, a simple truth changed my perspective: Once we have trusted Christ as Savior, He is alive and active in us. Jesus knows we are inadequate to live the Christian life on our own, so His Spirit indwells us to live His life in and through us. In this way Jesus can demonstrate His character through us to the watching world. Our responsibility is to surrender to Him.

"To them God has chosen to make known among the Gentiles the glorious riches of this mystery, which is Christ in you, the hope of glory." (Colossians 1:27 NIV)

January 7

Trust in The Lord

Cast your cares on the Lord and He will sustain you; He will never let the righteous fall.
Psalm 55:22 NIV

We are quick to affirm our faith in God's "saving grace," but we're not as sure about His "sustaining grace." How can we doubt His power to sustain us today and yet be assured of His salvation through eternity?

"Whoever believes in the Son has eternal life." (John 3:36a NIV)

"He who has the Son has life." (1 John 5:12a NIV)

"And my God will meet all your needs, according to his glorious riches in Christ Jesus." (Philippians 4:19 NIV)

What is the key to experiencing God's "sustaining grace" daily? "Cast your cares on the Lord." I must acknowledge my dependence upon Him and seek His help.

We are often like the small child who says, "I can do it myself." Sometimes God allows us to try so He can teach us His ways.

January 8

Wait on The Lord

I wait for the Lord, my soul waits and in His Word I put my hope.
Psalm 130:5 NIV

The believer needs to know how important timing is in the Christian life. God's ways are not our ways and His timing is not according to our timing. He has created time for mankind—not for His working.

Learning to wait o god is a discipline that most of us do not like to practice. It is a carry-over, the human spirit of independence, expressed in the Garden of Eden. Only as we are willing to accept our dependence on God, day by day, are we willing to wait for His direction and experience His best for our lives.

God often uses the waiting period to change attitudes, motives and to strengthen our faith.
God is faithful—He is never late!

"Be still before the Lord and wait patiently for Him."
(Psalm 37:7a NIV)

Practice a life style of waiting on the Lord through:

Faith—trusting God when no solution is in sight.

Humility—completely dependent on the Lord.

Patience—God is who He says He is. He will do what He says He will do.

Courage—Resist pressure from schedules or other people.

January 9

God's Will

Avoid every kind of evil.
I Thessalonians 5:22 NIV

We cannot avoid every kind of evil, because we live in a sinful world. But we can refuse to give evil a foothold by avoiding tempting situations and seek to obey God.

God must be involved in every part of our lives. We cannot separate our spiritual lives from everything else. We belong to Christ and He must be in control of our entire being. He is faithful and he will enable us to be all He has called us to be.

"God, who has called you into fellowship with His Son, Jesus Christ, our Lord, is faithful." (1 Corinthians 11:9)

God's purpose in calling me is that I become conformed to the image of Christ. He will never lead me into temptation, sin or disobedience. When I yield to sin He will forgive me if I confess my sin and repent.
(1 John 1:9-10)

"And God is faithful; he will not let you be tempted beyond what you can bear, but when you are tempted, he will also provide a way out so that you can stand up under it." (1 Corinthians 10:13b)

January 10

Wisdom

Oh, how I love your law! I meditate on it all day long.
Your commands make me wiser than my enemies, for
they are ever with me.
Psalm 119:97-98 NIV

We are given spiritual discernment in order to make wise judgments but we must choose to develop this gift. We do this by studying scripture. In the Bible God reveals who He is and how He works, so that we can rightly judge what is—and what is not—of Him.

Spiritual growth, like physical growth, is a long-term process. We develop wisdom over time through study, prayer and observation of God's principles in action. Spiritual discernment enables us to distinguish between right and wrong, good and best and between God's will and personal desires.

As part of the Trinity, the Holy Spirit knows the mind of God, and since He indwells me He also knows my thoughts. With this knowledge, He directs me toward decisions in line with God's will.

The scriptural principles I learn through the preaching of God's Word, and personal study, forms a grid which filters everything I see, hear and experience. Any untruth, entering the grid, sets off an alarm in my spirit. For this reason I must saturate my mind with scriptural truth.

January 11

Discernment

And this is my prayer: that your love may abound more and more in knowledge and depth of insight, so that you may be able to discern what is best, and may be pure and blameless until the day of Christ.
Philippians 1:9-10 NIV

Things are not always what they seem to be, therefore, I must not make decisions according to my feelings or judge situations based on what appears to be real. Some things that are neither wrong nor sinful, may be outside of God's will.

Scripture may not speak specifically to my situation, but it is filled with principles, and with the guidance of the Holy Spirit I can make the right judgments. The question is not whether a certain choice looks good or feels right, but whether or not it is God's will for me at that point of my life.

I need the mind of Christ so that I can evaluate situations from His perspective.

Spiritual discernment protects us from deception. It is our God-given capacity to judge what is right and wrong. Ignoring an agitation in our spirit ("spiritual static") is a step onto the pathway of sin.

I must make prayer, repentance and biblical training a part of my daily routine.

January 12

Motives

And you, my son Solomon, acknowledge the God of your father, and serve him with whole hearted devotion and with a willing mind, for the Lord searches every heart and understands every motive behind the thoughts.
1 Chronicles 28:9a NIV

Noting is hidden from God. He sees and understands everything in our heart. This should cause joy, not fear, because God knows even the worst about us and loves us anyway.

This is a sobering thought because there are so many thoughts going through my mind during the day and even during the night, in my subconscious mind. Many of these disturb me and I don't like to deal with them. I need God's discernment to distinguish between His leading and my desires. I need a spirit of discipline to deny self, love others and obey Him.

Lord, I'm dependent upon you day by day,
To direct me in your will and way.
Teach me the truth in your precious Word;
For wisdom and discernment to follow you, Lord.

January 13

God's Ways

He made known his ways to Moses, his deeds to the people of Israel. Psalm 103:7 NIV

Make me know your ways, O Lord. Psalm 25:4 NASB

It is important to understand the difference between God's ways and God's acts or deeds.

God's acts are the things He does in our lives or in creation—for example, we see Him answering prayer, healing diseases and providing for needs.

But God's ways are His motivations, reason and principles that cause Him to act in the way He does. God revealed His power to Israel as He worked miracles among them, providing and protecting them. He allowed Moses to understand the motives and principles behind his working, which has to do with wisdom and discernment.

"The Lord confides (trust, has confidence) in those who fear (reverence) Him and He makes His covenant (ways, words and promises) known to them." (Psalm 25:14 NASB)

Out God is a personal God who delights in fellowship with His children.

January 14

God's Will

*Be very careful, then, how you live—not as unwise but
as wise, making the most of every opportunity, because
the days are evil Therefore do not be foolish, but
understand what the Lord's will is.*

Ephesians 5:15-17 NIV

God has a moral will that applies to all of us. He has
given us clear requirements, in Scripture, for living a
God-honoring life. These include:

> Proper sexual behavior (1 Thessalonians 4:3)
> A thankful attitude (1 Thessalonians 5:18)
> A forgiving mindset (Ephesians 4:32)
> A servant's heart (Galatians 5:13)
> Involvement in a local church (Hebrews 10:25)

God has a personal will designed for each of us, beginning
at birth. Our personalities, abilities, vocation, marital
status and life span are a part of His plan.

God has a right to plan my life. He fashioned me in
the womb, He sustains me (causes my heart to give
life), and causes my body to function. He rescued me
from sin (death). He is my Counselor (gives wisdom
and understanding). He is my Provider (knows what
is best and gives me what I need).

God committed to making clear to every believer the plan for his or her life. The primary source for God's revelation is His Word. (Romans 12:1-2) The more time spent in reading and meditating on God's Word, the better equipped we are to make daily decisions in a way that brings honor to God.

God invests Himself, through His Holy Spirit, in His children's lives to bring fulfillment of His plan. (Proverbs 3:5-6)

January 15

Comfort

*Praise be to the God and Father of our Lord Jesus
Christ, the Father of compassion and the God of all
comfort, who comforts us in all our troubles, so that we
can comfort those in any trouble with the comfort we
ourselves have received from God.*
2 Corinthians 1:3-4

We may think when God comforts us, our troubles should go away. If that were always true then we would only turn to Him to be relieved of pain and not out of love for Him. Being comforted can also mean receiving strength, encouragement and hope to deal with our problems. As we endure the trials we are better prepared to comfort and encourage others who are going through similar experiences.

Never, never forget—God is in control!

Nothing can touch my life unless it comes through the permissive will of God—He causes it or allows it. I cannot control circumstances but I can control how I will respond to them. I can choose to allow God to work through my circumstances for what is best in my life, and those around me, or I can rebel and try to be in control myself. God will allow me to make the choice—to help or hinder His plans.

Only when I acknowledge my dependence upon Him, and wait patiently for His plans, can I find peace and contentment.

January 16

Chosen in Christ

*For he chose us in him before the creation of the
world to be holy and blameless in his sight. In love
he predestined us to be adopted as his sons through
Jesus Christ, in accordance with his pleasure and will.
Ephesians 1:4-5*

Volumes have been written trying to explain this verse.
We need to consider what Paul is saying and why he is
saying it. He is talking about the spiritual blessings we
have in Christ.

Before we existed, God originated His plan of redemption—His Son, the Lord Jesus Christ, the Lamb slain before the foundation of the world, would be sacrificed to pay
the penalty for mankind's sin. He would elect (choose)
those who accepted His Son as their substitute in death.

Election has to do with people—whosoever will accept
Jesus is chosen and whosoever won't accept Jesus is
not chosen. Individual salvation depends on individual
choice. Predestination has to do with purpose—the
purpose God has for us after salvation. His purpose
for our salvation is to accept us as His children (John
1:12), that we might become like (conformed to) His
beloved Son, Jesus. (Romans 9:28-29)

When we accept Jesus as our Savior we can know
(Ephesians 1:11) that God has chosen us and His
purpose will be fulfilled.

You don't have to work for it, you don't have to worry
about it—it is guaranteed! (Ephesians 1:13)

January 17

Affliction

*It was good for me to be afflicted so that I might learn
your decrees. The law from your mouth is more precious
to me than thousands of pieces of silver or gold.*

Psalm 119:71-72

Are you going through the valley of trials and
tribulations; wondering why God is allowing adverse
situations in your life? Be assured that God knows what
is going on and He has a purpose for what is happening.
We have a choice as to how we will respond—we can
become bitter or better.

Our affliction may be health, finances, family or any
way He chooses to get our attention. If we ignore His
"still small voice" He will continue, in other ways, until
He gets our attention in what we need to learn.

For the Psalmist, it was to learn His decrees (His ways,
His works and His will). When we turn to the Lord,
seeking with our whole heart, He will teach us what we
need to know and show us where we need to go.

Only then, will His peace fill our heart.

January 18

Commitment

*Love the Lord your God with all your heart and with all
your soul and with all your strength.*
Deuteronomy 6:5 NIV

This is what life is all about—my relationship with God
from beginning through eternity. I am to express my
love to God with my total being. My being involves my
body, soul and spirit.

> Body—physical strength
> Soul—mind, emotions, will
> Spirit—heart

God must be a part of my everyday life, every aspect
and experience must include Him—not just church-
related activities. "...for I, the Lord your God, am a
jealous god." (Deuteronomy 5:9) God is vigilant in
guarding our love for Him.

Since we were created to love the Lord and to be loved
by Him, anything that competes for our devotion will
hinder us in His purpose and plan for our life.

January 19

God's Work in Us

*And we know that in all things God works for the good
of those who love him, who have been called according to
his purpose.*
Romans 8:28

If we could choose, none of us would ask for difficulties
in our life. Yet God sees value in troublesome times.
He uses trials to accomplish His plans. He can work
good through the bad situations in our life.

One of God's purposes for us is a growing intimacy in
our relationship with Him. We can easily get caught up
in so many other things, that occupy our time, and we
neglect our time with the Lord. He can use hardships
to get our attention.

God also desires to conform us to the image of Christ.
He often uses pain to bring areas of ungodliness to the
surface, where we can deal with them in confession
and repentance.

Stressful circumstances are a good tool to test our
faith. It is easy to say, "God is good" when things are
going well but how trustful are we when trials and
tribulations come?

Do we come through with a deeper intimacy, stronger
faith and more godly character? This is God's purpose.

January 20

As a Child

When I was a child, I talked like a child, I thought like a child, I reasoned like a child. When I became a man, I put childish ways behind me.

I Corinthians 13:11 NIV

Paul includes this thought in his special chapter on love. Why? What does childish behavior have to do with love? It's usually about self. (Me, myself and I.) God's love is about others and it is always unconditional.

As children we learn many things, which may or may not be accurate. These beliefs form a "grid" through which we interpret life.

An example of immature thinking: performance is necessary for acceptance and love. That success equals approval or love is dependent upon achievement. As we grow up we may continue to think this way. If we do it can affect our relationship with God and others. We become performance oriented, considering acceptance as dependent on performance. We may allow the same idea to spill over in our expectations of others.

We must put away our childish way of thinking and practice the mind of Christ in our love and acceptance of others.

January 21

God's Way

Delight yourself in the Lord and he will give you the desires of your heart.
Psalm 37:4

If the Lord delights in a man's way, he makes his steps firm; though he stumble, he will not fall, for the Lord upholds him with his hand.
Psalm 37:23-24

To delight in someone means to experience great joy and pleasure in the presence of that person. This happens when we know that person well. To delight in the Lord means we should know Him better. We need to know His ways, His will, His works, His love, His grace and forgiveness.

God delights in the one who follows, trusts and obeys him (v. 5). If I want God to direct my way then I must seek His advice before I step out.

To claim these promises, I must consider the context in which they are written. I am told to trust in the Lord, do good and be faithful (v. 3). If I truly pursue God's desires then my desires will fall into place with His will.

Then I am to "rest in the Lord and wait patiently for Him." (v. 7). His timing is always perfect.

January 22

Obedience

But Samuel replied; Does the Lord delight in burnt offerings and sacrifices as much as in obeying the voice of the Lord? To obey is better than sacrifice, and to heed is better than the fat of rams.

I Samuel 15:22

Anything I do for the Lord is empty unless I do it with an attitude of love and obedience, in my heart. I show my love for God through my obedience to Him in what He has commanded me to do. He looks into the heart—the motive—before He considers what I do outwardly.

God wants us to love Him, trust Him, and turn from our sins; after that He will be pleased with our time, money and service.

Parents delight in their children when they do what they've been asked to do. In the same way, God delights in His children when they do what he has asked them to do.

Doing good to impress other people does not honor God. My faithfulness will depend upon spending time with God and seeking His will daily.

January 23

Fear

The Lord is my light and my salvation—whom shall I fear? The Lord is the stronghold of my life—of whom shall I be afraid?

Psalm 27:1 NIV

Fear is a dark shadow that covers us and imprisons us within ourselves. Each of us has experienced fear at sometime in our life and most of us many times. Fear of rejection, uncertainty, making a mistake, sickness, death.

Fear can cause us to miss God's best because we fail to step out on faith. Fear can affect us physically, emotionally and spiritually. We may become so anxious that we are unable to make simple decisions. This affects the choices we make and thus it controls our lives.

The solution—faith and trust in the Lord. He has promised to direct us when we trust Him. (Proverbs 3:5-6)

January 24

Fear

For I am the Lord, your God, who takes hold of your right hand and says to you, do not fear; I will help you.
Isaiah 41:13

The picture here is of God walking with me, holding my right hand with His left hand. In verse 10 of this chapter the Lord says, "I will uphold you with my right hand."

With His left hand He holds me and with His right He protects me, what security! "Thy right hand, O Lord, is become glorious in power; thy right hand, O Lord, hath dashed in pieces the enemy." (Exodus 15:6)

I have often reminded God of His promise in Isaiah 41:10, by praying it back to Him, and then trusting Him to be faithful to His promise.

Trusting God is the only way to be free from fear.

January 25

Wisdom

The fear of the Lord is the beginning of knowledge, but fools despise wisdom and discipline.

Proverbs 1:7

"A wise man learns from another man's mistake, a fool learns from his own."

No one likes to be called a fool but all of us meet some during our lifetime. If we are honest, we may have acted like a fool at some time.

One of the most annoying types of people is a know-it-all, who refuses to learn and resents any type of advice. Solomon calls such a person a fool.

Today, information and knowledge is plentiful but wisdom is scarce. Few honor and respect God and fewer obey His Word. Wisdom comes from God and when He is ignored there can be no true understanding that will guide our attitudes and actions.

Remember, only God knows it all but we can learn from one another. "To learn, we must listen more and talk less, for we already know what we would say."

"Wisdom is the mind of God revealed." For the Lord gives wisdom, and from His mouth come knowledge and understanding. (Proverbs 2:6)

January 26

Obedience

Then Jesus said to his disciples, If anyone would come after me, he must deny himself, and take up his cross and follow me.
Matthew 16:24

Our natural tendency is to avoid self-sacrifice and suffering. Both of these may be involved in obedience. Self-service is the enemy of obedience. If I seek to obey God's will, then I must deny myself anything that does not fit in with His plan. It may be something that is not wrong for anyone else but it just isn't in God's will for me.

Self-denial (death to self) has to do with my desire and ambitions that interfere with my service to the Lord. My attitude must be like that of the Lord Jesus Christ: "Not my will but yours, (Father) be done." (Luke 22:42)

When I submit to God's will, I will then find peace in my commitment.

January 27

God's Faithfulness

*Jesus Christ is the same yesterday and today and
forever. Hebrews 13:8*

*For I, the Lord, do not change.
Malachi 3:6*

In a changing world I can trust my unchanging Lord.
The foundation of our faith is based on the truth that
God is unchanging. In order for the Lord to lay a solid
faith foundation in our lives, we must study the one we
serve.

Through the Scriptures and our experiences we learn
how God responds to different circumstances. We
recognize His method and purpose for discipline, and
we witness His rewarding of righteousness.

We also know that He is always the same Loving
Father.

Any unfair, unloving or dishonest action cannot come
from God.

"Righteousness and justice are the foundation of your
throne; love and faithfulness go before you." (Psalm
89:14)

Revival

If my people, who are called by my name, will humble themselves and pray and seek my face and turn from their wicked ways, then will I hear from heaven and will forgive their sin and will heal their land.

II Chronicles 7:14

This promise was made to Israel, through Solomon, in answer to his prayer that God would make provision for the people when they sinned. As God's people we can make application in similar situations.

God answered with four conditions for forgiveness:

1) Humble ourselves by admitting our sins. (Psalm 51:17) Pride will hinder revival. God desires a broken and contrite heart.

2) Pray—confession brings forgiveness. (1 John 1:9)

3) Seek God's face—(Jeremiah 29:13). Don't seek solutions, seek the "problem Solver."

4) Turn from sin—Repentance (Jeremiah 31:19). No forsaking, no revival.

The result—favor, fellowship, fruitfulness.

"Revival cannot be worked up; it can only be prayed down."

"Revival: A new beginning of obedience to God."
                                        Charles Finney

January 29

Praise

*Great is the Lord and most worthy of praise; his
greatness no one can fathom.*
Psalm 145:3

Praise is a celebration of the Lord—recalling His
faithfulness to His promises, His ways and His works.
Praise focuses our attention on God—not self.

When we are going through troubled times it is not
easy to praise the Lord. We must remember that God
is in control and every trial that enters our life comes
through his permissive will. Whatever His reason for
allowing it, He is faithful to see us through it.

We limit our praise through a lack of knowledge of God
and His ways. Only through His Word can we know His
attributes and promises. Genuine praise also involves
giving glory to God—this is our worship,

We cannot truly claim to understand praise until we
have experienced it for ourselves through faith.

> Praise the Lord, ye heavens adore Him,
> Praise Him all ye men on earth.
> God incarnate came from Glory;
> Identified with man through the Virgin Birth.

January 30

Knowing God

For I delight in loyalty rather than sacrifice, and in the knowledge of God rather than burnt offerings.

Hosea 6:6

God wants us to know Him. That's why he has gone to great lengths to reveal Himself—through His Word and through His Son, the Lord Jesus Christ. Knowing about God is one thing but knowing God is another. Anyone can learn some facts about Him but knowing Him takes time and effort to become His friend.

By reading the Bible we can accumulate facts about God's character, principles and His plan and purpose for creation. That's just the beginning. We then need to meditate on the Scripture—think about His words and allow the Holy Spirit to interpret His truth. Finally, we need to apply what we learn.

Example: 46:1 (Psalm)

We read that God is a very present help in time of trouble. Then, when trouble comes we rely on Him for help. When we experience that help we learn something—He is faithful, and we learn to practice faith in our daily life.

God wants our attention more than gifts or works. Often we focus our attention on our works for the Lord more than our worship of the Lord. Prayer and meditation involve time and effort of self, heart searching and confession. It is often more convenient to give a gift or do a good deed that others will notice. It's more gratifying to the flesh, but less nourishing to the Spirit.

January 31

Christian Living

Go I say, live by the Spirit and you will not gratify the desires of the sinful nature (v. 16). But the fruit of the Spirit is love, joy, peace, patience, kindness, goodness, faithfulness, gentleness, and self-control.

Galatians 5:16, 22

Being led by the Spirit involves the desire to hear, the readiness to obey God's Word, and the sensitivity to discern between my feelings and His promptings. When I seek to be guided by the Holy Spirit, the words of Christ will be in my mind, the love of Christ will be behind my actions and the power of Christ will help me control my selfish desires.

The fruit of the Spirit is the spontaneous work of the Holy Spirit in us. The Spirit produces these character traits that are found in the nature of Christ. They are the by-product of Christ's control. We can't obtain them by trying to get them without His help. We must daily commit our sinful nature to God's control and draw on the Spirit's power to overcome it. I must not let anything or anyone else influence my values or standards in any area of my life. "God's Spirit is the believer's internal motivation for expressing external evidence of faith."

February

February 1

Bitterness

Get rid of all bitterness, rage and anger, brawling and slander along with every form of malice. Be kind and compassionate to one another, forgiving each other, just as in Christ God forgave you.

Ephesians 4:31-32

Sin always blocks our vision of God and hinders our fellowship with Him. Our perception of people and situations become blurred and our attitudes are influenced by what we see and hear rather than what God's Word says.

A right relationship with God leads to a right relationship with others, especially fellow believers. We may not feel loving toward them but we are to pursue peace as we become more Christ like.

A "bitterroot" grows if we fail to deal with any sinful attitudes of resentment, anger, jealousy and it will influence those around us.

"Bitterness is a toxin we prepare for someone else, but then drink it our self."

The antidote is "forgiveness"—just as in Christ God forgave you.

February 2

Time With God

O God, You are my God; early will I seek You; my soul
thirsts for You; my flesh longs for You in a dry and
thirsty land where there is no water.
Psalm 63:1 NKJV

Daily devotions are more about progress than perfection. There are no perfect circumstances to have quality "quiet time," with the Lord. There may be no "outward distractions" but what about "inner distractions?" God can control the outward but I have a responsibility for the inward—the struggle between the flesh and the Spirit.

Devotions are a matter of the heart's desire more than discipline of our time. When we long to be with God we experience His presence and person in a special way as He reveals His will. In a mysterious way, as we spend time with God, "beholding as in a mirror the glory of the Lord, (we) are being transformed into the same image." (II Corinthians 3:18) I find that spending time with God actually changes the kind of person I am.

February 3

Faith

These have come so that your faith—of greater worth than gold, which perishes even though refined by fire—may be proved genuine and may result in praise, glory and honor when Jesus Christ is revealed.

I Peter 1:7

My faith is more precious than gold. Why? The more gold I spend the less I have. Not so with my faith—the more I use it the stronger it becomes. Gold doesn't begin bright and shiny as we know it to be. It has to be refined by fire and crafted by tools. In the same way God sends trials into my life to shape me into the likeness of Christ. These tools vary but they are used to transform me and build my faith.

I have a choice to accept or reject His transforming work in my life but He will return to a faith area, that needs His attention, until I finally submit. He loves me too much to let me remain in my imperfect condition.

My faith is precious to God. His work is sometimes painful but He is always there to help me through the process. We can't really know the depth of our character until we see how we act under pressure. It's easy to be kind to others when all is going well, but can we still be kind when others are treating us unfairly?

February 4

Faith

Now the just shall live by faith: but if any man draw
back, my soul shall have no pleasure in him.
Hebrews 10:38

Two words describe faith: Sure and certain. These two qualities need a secure beginning and ending point.

The beginning point of faith is believing in God's character—He is who He says He is.

The ending point is believing in God's promises—He will do what He says He will do.

When we believe that God will fulfill His promises even though we don't see those promises materializing yet, we demonstrate true faith. (John 20:29)

Believing that God exists is only the beginning; even the demons believe that. (James 2:19-20) God will not settle for mere acknowledgement of His existence. He wants a personal relationship with you that will transform your life. Those who seek God will find they are rewarded with His intimate presence.

Exercising faith is not being passive- folding hands and waiting for God to do something—we must follow His leading and obey His Word.

February 5

Temptation

So, if you think you're standing firm, be careful that you don't fall!
I Corinthians 10:12

Temptation is a process—and processes can be stopped at any stage. Temptation usually begins in the mind and that's where Satan sends his fiery darts to entice us. The mind has the capacity to enable us to live in a fantasy world. If we allow our self to dwell in this "fantasy thinking," we can become enslaved. We then begin to entertain thoughts of making it a reality.

Wherever we go or whatever we do we can never outrun our mind. What we can do is disrupt the process by filling our mind with the Word of God. His Word is truth. His Word is powerful. It will cut right through the fantasy and reality so we can overcome the temptation,

God is faithful and He will not allow us to be tempted beyond what we are able to bear (v. 13).

February 6

Temptation

When tempted no one should say, 'God is tempting me.'
For God cannot be tempted by evil, nor does he tempt
anyone; but each one is tempted when by his own evil
desire, he is dragged away and enticed.

James 1:13-14

Human nature always tries to lead us to blame someone else for our mistakes. It started with Adam and Eve. Adam blamed Eve and Eve blamed the serpent, but it is a personal choice when we yield to our desires.

Temptation is toward evil and Satan is the Tempter. Testing is toward good and God uses it to refine our faith and to help us grow in our dependence on Christ, who is our strength. (Philippians 4:13)

Temptation is not sin—yielding is.

Christ was tempted—He did not yield.

He answered Satan with the Word of God and we have that same Word to use as our defense against the Tempter.

February 7

No Other Name

Salvation is found in no one else, for there is no other name under heaven given to men by which we must be saved.

Acts 4:12

Many people react negatively to the fact that there is no other name than that of Jesus to call on for salvation. This is not something the Church decided; it is a specific teaching of Jesus Himself. (John 14:6) Since God designated Jesus to be the Savior of the world, no one else can be His equal.

Christians can be open-minded on some issues but not on how we are saved from sin. No other religious teacher could die for our sins. No other religious teacher came to earth as God's only Son; no other religious teacher rose from the dead. Our focus should be on Jesus, whom God offered as a way to have an eternal relationship with Himself. There is no other name or way.

February 8

Knowing God

I keep asking that the God of our Lord Jesus Christ, the glorious Father, may give you the Spirit of wisdom and revelation, so that you may know Him better.
Ephesians 1:17

Jesus became such a real human being that God was His God just as much as He is our God. It is only through the Lord Jesus that this God can be fully known and approached. He is the only one who bridged the gulf between God and man.

He is the God of our Lord Jesus Christ.
He is the Father of our Lord Jesus Christ. (Ephesians 1:3)
He is the glorious Father—the "Father of glory."
Jesus is the "Lord of glory." (I Corinthians 2:8)
Holy Spirit is the "revealer of glory." (I Corinthians 2:9, 10)

Glory is all wrapped up in the Trinity.
        The origin of glory—the Father
        The source of glory—the Holy Spirit
        The king of glory—Christ, the Son

We can know God in the glory of His person, and His personality as He reveals Himself to us. He has chosen to make Himself known in two ways—His Written Word and His Living Word.

He has said what He is like in His Written Word and He has shown what He is like in His Living Word.

God's Glory—His Eternal Perfections

February 9

Son of God

*For in him dwelleth all the fullness of the Godhead
bodily, and ye are complete in him, which is the head of
all principality and power.*

Colossians 2:9-10a

The Christian life has two sides—on one side I am complete in Christ (sealed and secure in Him). On the other hand I am growing in Christ (becoming more like Him). I feel the presence of Christ and the pressure of sin. I enjoy the peace of God but still face daily problems that help me grow.

Faith, hope and love are at the heart of life in Christ. It begins with <u>faith</u> in the death of Christ that has delivered me from the past. It grows in <u>hope</u> as I learn all that God has in mind for me –promise of the future. God's <u>love</u> is shed abroad in my heart as I reach out to others.

The love that caused Christ to die is the same love that sends the Holy Spirit to live in me to guide me every day. The power that raised Christ from the dead is the same power that saved me and is available to me daily. God's power and love is available to help me face every challenge or trial.

February 10

Obedience

Jesus replied, If any one loves me, he will obey my teaching. My Father will love him, and we will come to him and make our home with him.

John 14:23

I don't have to know the future to have faith in God; I have to have faith in God to be secure about the future.

Love is more than words. It is commitment and conduct. God does not separate loving Him and obeying Him. What commands are we to obey? Jesus summed them up into one command: "Love the Lord your God with all your heart and with all your soul and with all your mind," and "Love your neighbor as yourself." (Matthew 22:37, 39)

As we study the Word, the Holy Spirit will reveal how to live out these commands. As we follow His leading, we are saying, "I love you," to God. If we do what He wants us to do, we will be what He wants us to be.

"We know that we have come to know him if we obey his commands." (I John 2:3)

The proof of this is not in emotions or exciting worship, but in the daily, detailed, disciplined obedience by which our character is being transformed into the image of Christ. When we obey Him, showing our genuine love to Him, His love will overflow in our lives.

February 11

Sin

My dear children, I write this to you so that you will not sin. But if anybody does sin, we have one who speaks to the Father in our defense –Jesus Christ, the Righteous One.
I John 2:1

My case is no longer on the docket for Jesus paid the penalty on Calvary and set me free. His death satisfied the wrath of God against sin. I will never attain a state of sinless perfection, this side of heaven, but it can always be my goal.

"I'm not what I ought to be, but I'm not what I once was. And it is by the grace of God that I am what I am." John Newton

An authentic Christian is one who knows who Christ is and he trusts what Christ did. The two natures of Jesus Christ, humanity ad deity, are brought together. In life and in eternity, He is perfection personified!

"Jesus Christ, the Righteous One"
"Son of God and God the Son"

February 12

Wisdom

If any of you lacks wisdom, he should ask God—and it will be given him.

James 1:5

For the Lord gives wisdom, and from his mouth come knowledge and understanding.

Proverbs 2:6

Wisdom comes in two ways: it is a God-given gift and also the result of our serious search. Wisdom's starting point is God and His revealed Word, the source of knowledge and understanding. In that sense wisdom is His gift to us. But he gives it only to those who seek it. He does not give it to the rebellious and foolish.

Christians don't have to grope in the dark for answers, we can ask God for wisdom to make the right choices. Wisdom begins with respect for God, leads to right living and the ability to tell right from wrong.

To learn God's will we need to read His Word and ask Him to show us how to obey it. Then we must do what He tells us.

February 13

Doubt

But when he asks, he must believe and not doubt,
because he who doubts is like a wave of the sea, blown
and tossed by the wind.

James 1:6

To believe and not doubt means not only believing in the existence of God but also believing in His loving care, and that He will hear and answer our prayer.

Jesus said, "If you believe, you will receive whatever you ask for in prayer." (Matthew 21:22)

This verse is not a guarantee that we can get anything we want just by asking Jesus and believing. God does not grant requests that would hurt us or anyone else or that would violate His nature or will. Our request must be in harmony with the principles in His Word.

As we grow in grace and knowledge of our Lord Jesus Christ, the more likely our prayers will be in line with God's will and then God will be happy to grant them.

A mind that wavers is not convinced that God's way is best. It shifts back and forth between feelings, the world's ideas and God's commands. If you want to stop being tossed about, ask God for wisdom and trust that He will give it to you. Then your decisions will be sure and solid.

February 14

Son of God

No one has ever seen God, but God the One and Only,
who is at the Father's side, has made Him known.

John 1:18

"God, the One and Only" is a title showing that Jesus is both God and the Father's unique Son. In Christ, God revealed His nature and person in a way that could be seen and touched. In Christ, God became a man that lived on earth. He identified with mankind, in his humanity, being tempted in ways that we are tempted, yet He did not yield to temptation. (Hebrews 4:5) There was no sin in Him, therefore He was the perfect sacrifice to pay for the sin of mankind.

Through His blood we can be forgiven, justified and reconciled with a Holy God, when we accept Jesus' death as our death to sin and through faith enter an eternal relationship with God.

February 15

Death

For to me, to live is Christ and to die is gain.
Philippians 1:2

Paul's consuming desire was to magnify the Lord Jesus Christ in his body—to be an extension of the presence of Christ, an expression of the person of Christ and to exhibit the power of Christ—whether in life or death. He had experienced much pain and pressure in his ministry. He also experienced paradise (whether in the body or out of the body; II Corinthians 12:2-4) which he was not allowed to share.

We don't know what was involved in that revelation to Paul but his desire was to be where God wanted him to be, doing what God wanted him to do.

God has not chosen to give us a full revelation of life after death, only some brief descriptions in His Word. We do know that while we are still here on earth, Christ is with us, in the person of His Holy Spirit indwelling the Believer, and when we die we will be with Him in person. We will move from faith to sight. (II Corinthians 5:6-8)

February 16

Death

Just as man is destined to die once, and after that to face judgment, so Christ was sacrificed once to take away the sins of many people; and he will appear a second time, not to bear sin, but to bring salvation to those who are waiting for him.

Hebrews 9:27-28

All people die physically, but Christ died so we would not have to die spiritually. Consider this thought: All who are born twice will die once. Those born once will die twice.

We can have true confidence in the saving work of Christ for us, doing away with sin—past, present and future. He has forgiven our past sin—when He died on the cross, he sacrificed Himself once for all. (Hebrews 9:26)

He has given us the Holy Spirit to help us deal with present sins—He is in heaven as our High Priest. (Hebrews 9:24)

He promises to return and raise us to eternal life where there will be no sin. (Hebrews 9:28)

February 17

Salvation

*Therefore he is able to save completely (or forever) those
who come to God through him.*
Hebrews 7:25

No one can add to what Jesus did to save us; our past, present and future sins are all forgiven. Jesus is with the Father as a sign that our sins are forgiven. He is our mediator (our high priest), our intercessor continually before the Father, concerned for our interest.

By his blood alone we have our conscience cleansed. We are freed from the sting of death and the power of sin.

Jesus understands our struggles because He faced the same, as a human being, while on earth. We can trust Him to help us overcome temptation. Christ is on our side at God's side. He is our Lord and Savior. He is there to present both our needs and our service for Him, as an offering.

Most of us are not aware of how the Lord is working in our daily life. However, He is active all the time moving in circumstances, through the prayers of His children, changing situations for our good and His glory.

February 18

Righteous Living

*Do not offer the parts of your body to sin, as instruments
of wickedness, but rather offer yourselves to God—and
offer the parts of your body to him as instruments of
righteousness.*

Romans 6:13

When we accept Christ as Lord, we are His and no
longer free to do as we please with our bodies, in which
His Holy Spirit dwells. I believe that we, as Christians,
do not fully accept this truth. We still want to be in
control of our body according to the pattern of the
world.

Our idea of salvation involves only our soul and spirit
and our uppermost thought is Heaven when we die.
God's plan is for our good, here on earth also, but for
this to become a reality we must renew our mind to
think on His will and ways.

For God to use the parts of our body, as instruments
of righteousness, involves our character, conduct and
conversation; who we are, what we do and what we say.

Spiritual life and physical life cannot be separated. We
must respect our body and care for it so God can use it
for His glory.

February 19

God's Word

Then Jesus said, He who has ears to hear, let him hear.
Mark 4:9

Jesus had just shared the" Parable of the Four Soils" with his disciples. He explained it as representing the different ways people respond to the Word of God. The state of mind with which we listen to God's Word determines how we grow.

We hear with our ears but there is a different, deeper kind of hearing with our mind and heart that is necessary in order to gain spiritual understanding of God's truth. Some don't understand because they are not ready for it. Seekers hear and understand. The result depends upon the condition of the soil.

4 Types of Soil: (Mark 4:1-20)

1. Path—closed mind—choose not to hear—Satan snatches away the truth.

2. Rocky—cloudy mind—received with joy—no root—never nurtured.

3. Thorns—cluttered mind—worldly cares and misplaced values—no room for God.

4. Good soil—committed mind—received truth, produced fruit

February 20

Prayer

*In him and through faith in him we may approach God
with freedom and confidence.*
Ephesians 3:12

Fellowship with God at anytime, any place, is mine
through faith in Christ, who sits at God's right hand. I
have freedom through His death and confidence through
His resurrection. I am welcome in His presence. He is
more willing and longing for me to come to Him, than
I am willing to meet with Him.

"So do not throw away your confidence; it will be richly
rewarded. You need to persevere so that when you
have done the will of God, you will receive what He has
promised." (Hebrews 10:35-36)

Faith means resting in what God has done for us in the
past, but it also means trusting in Him for what He will
do in the present and the future.

I will never take lightly the prayers of others on my
behalf. My attitude and motive may hinder my prayers
and God may choose to work through the prayers of
someone else to accomplish His will in my life. In the
same way, I should never underestimate my prayers on
behalf of others.

February 21

Humility

All of you, clothe yourselves with humility toward one another, because God opposes the proud but gives grace to the humble.

1 Peter 5:5

What Peter is really saying is "cover yourselves up with humility if you expect to be blessed with God's grace." Many of us have a problem with humility because it goes against our human nature. We're like the deacon who said to his pastor, "I'm so proud I've finally learned to be humble."

Solomon said, "Pride goes before destruction, a haughty spirit before a fall." (Proverbs 16:18)

This should be a warning for us. Pride led to Satan's downfall and ultimately to his destruction in Hell.

Humility: Recognizing my total dependence on God and seeking His will.

Hindrances: Impatience, insecurity, ignorance of God's ways (disregard for His Word), impure motives, impulsiveness, ingratitude.

God has His plans for my life and His way of fulfilling those plans. He's not as interested in the goal as He is in the process of reaching that goal. As I follow His leading day by day, step by step, He is being glorified and I am becoming more like Christ.

February 22

Heaven

*But our citizenship is in heaven, and we eagerly await a
Savior from there, the Lord Jesus Christ.*
Philippians 3:20

Some people are citizens of two different countries
here on earth—they have a dual citizenship and enjoy
the privileges of both countries.

As Christians we are temporarily residents on earth
but our true citizenship is in Heaven. Our Landlord
is preparing our dwelling place there, awaiting our
arrival. He's looking forward to our coming, (Psalm
116:15), and He will present us with a "crown of
righteousness" because we have been longing and
looking for His coming. (II Timothy 4:8)

What a day that will be! We cannot imagine all that He
has prepared for us (I Corinthians 2:9). "No eye has
seen, no ear has heard, no mind has conceived what
God has prepared for those who love Him."

Believing God's promises and knowing His faithfulness,
we can look beyond our tribulations here because we
have the hope, assurance, security and peace of eternity
with Jesus.

February 23

Evil

*For our struggle is not against flesh and blood, but
against the rulers, against the authorities, against the
powers of this dark world and against the spiritual
forces of evil in the heavenly realms.*
Ephesians 6:12

When we are faced with problems, our human nature immediately looks for someone to blame. Whether it is family, friend or foe, we focus our attention in that direction and decide how we're going to deal with it. How we respond can take care of the situation or make it worse. We need wisdom to make the right decision.

Paul says our struggle is not against people (flesh and blood), but against Satan and his forces of evil. We need to be more aware of him and his evil host and what God has provided for us to defeat him. His goal is to defeat Christ's Church and he will use any device he can think of to accomplish his goal.

As Believers we have the Holy Spirit indwelling us to enable us to overcome, through the name of Jesus, the blood of Jesus, the victory of Jesus and the Word of God. Jesus depended on the Holy Spirit and the Word to resist Satan and we can do the same. (James 4:7) Jesus' victory is ours to claim.

We are not told to fight, nor to run, but to "stand," dressed in the armor provided and pray. (Ephesians 6:8-10)

February 24

Peace

I have told you these things, so that in me you may have peace. In this world you will have trouble. But take heart! I have overcome the world.

John 16:33

Jesus summed up the things He had been telling His disciples, in preparation for His returning to the Father. He told them to take courage for they would not be alone. The Holy Spirit would minister His peace in their hearts. We have the same promise. (Philippians 4: 6, 7)

Many forces are at war in our hearts each day—sin, fear, uncertainty, doubt—but the peace of God moves into our heart to restrain these forces when we turn to Him in faith.

We have peace with God through the death and resurrection of our Lord Jesus Christ. We have the peace of God through the life of Christ and His intercession with the Father on our behalf.

February 25

Seeking God

This is what Hezekiah did throughout Judah, doing what was good and right and faithful before the Lord his God. In everything that he understood --- he sought his God and worked wholeheartedly. And so he prospered.

II Chronicles 31:20-21

One day God sent Hezekiah word to set his house in order for he was going to die. Hezekiah prayed and wept, reminding God of his faithfulness. God gave him fifteen more years. (II Kings 20:3)

What does it mean to seek God with our whole heart? God wants us intimately connected with Him. He is our Father—we are His children.

When we approach His Word with a distracted mind or pray with our focus drifting to other things, we have a divided heart. He deserves our full attention. We are totally dependent on Him for everything in life and He delights in revealing Himself and blessing us when our heart and mind is set on Him. (Hebrews 11:6)

"The most important thing in my life is not my service, winning people to Jesus, preaching sermons or being a pastor. The most important thing in my life is building my relationship with Christ." Oswald Chambers

February 26

Unity

I pray also for those who will believe in me through their message, that all of them may be one, Father, just as you are in me and I am in you. May they also be in us so that the world may believe that you have sent me.

John 17: 20-21

What is the greatest hindrance in evangelism today? It is not a lack of laborers, nor a lack of money. It is a lack of unity in the Body of Christ. Jesus prayed for unity among believers based on their unity with Him and the Father. Christians can know unity among themselves if they are living in union with God.

Jesus wanted His followers unified as a powerful witness to the reality of God's love. The love of God cannot be demonstrated through His church when there is conflict, contention and division among its members. The only way the love of God can be made known to the world is through Jesus, His Beloved Son, who was sent for that purpose.

When we become like Christ—conformed to His image (Romans 8:28-29), then we become true witnesses of God's love. (John 13:25)

February 27

Seeking God

*O God, you are my God, earnestly I seek you; my soul
thirsts for you, my body longs for you.*

Psalm 63:1

David was seeking God with all of his being—his whole
heart. He realized his total dependence upon God.
He longed for His presence, His provision and His
protection. (David was hiding from his enemies, in the
desert.)

Our total being involves our body, soul and spirit—
physical, emotional and spiritual—our soul involves
mind, emotions and will.

David was truly saying:

Earnestly I seek you (my spirit cries out for you).

*My soul thirsts for you (my mind needs your comfort, my
emotions need your peace, my will needs your direction).*

*My body longs for you (my body begs for your strength
and nourishment).*

We are no less dependent on God than David was. Maybe we are not as aware as David was but God desires
that we come to that awareness through a knowledge
of His Word.

Lord, give me seeing eyes and an understanding mind
to realize that all I am and all I have is because of
your love and goodness to me. I can do nothing or be
anything apart from you. Thank you.

February 28

Power of God

Now to him who is able to do immeasurably more than all we ask or imagine, according to his power that is at work within us, to him be glory in the church and in Christ Jesus throughout all generations, forever and ever! Amen

Ephesians 3:20-21

Paul says that God is able to do in us and through us what is impossible for the mind to comprehend, because of the power of the Holy Spirit indwelling us. This same power raised Jesus from the dead and also transformed my heart with new life. Christ is in me and I am in Christ - I am complete in Him for He has filled me with all the fullness of Himself.

Sometimes God can glorify Himself, in a greater way, through sustaining us in our trouble rather than delivering us out of it.

Never doubt the power of God in you or through you to accomplish His will.

Thank you, Lord; that your power is made perfect, in my weakness, when I let go and let you have your way in my life. Forgive me when I try to prove my strength and hinder you in your work.

February 29

Obedience

Why do you call me 'Lord, Lord,' and do not do what I say? Luke 6:46

Not everyone who says to me, 'Lord, Lord,' will enter the kingdom of heaven, but only he who does the will of my Father, who is in heaven.
Matthew 7:21

God is more interested in our walk than in our talk. It's easy to talk but hard to walk.

It has been said that profession without performance is pretense.

Jesus made the above statements while teaching about building on a solid foundation, in reference to the Christian life. Jesus, Himself is that foundation. The will of the Father is that we not only believe on the Lord Jesus Christ, as His Son, but we are to know and do what he says.

Accepting Jesus as our foundation may take only a moment but building on that foundation can take a lifetime of learning and obeying Him. Only through reading and meditating upon His Word, seeking his direction and obeying Him, can we know how to build on that foundation for eternity.

March

March 1

The Word

*Do not merely listen to the Word, and so deceive
yourselves. Do what it says.*
James 1:22

It is important to read and study the Word, but it is
much more important to obey it by doing what it says.
The purpose for knowing the Word is to know God, His
will and His ways, that we can be what He wants us to
be and do what He wants us to do.

The most important thing in my life is my relationship
with God. My concept of God will destroy or develop
that relationship. If the basis of my concept of God is
His word, then I can know Him as He is, for He reveals
Himself through His Word. His Written Word is the
truth about His Living Word, the Lord Jesus Christ.
"For in Him dwelleth all the fullness of the Godhead
bodily." (Colossians 2:9)

I can know His Word, His ways, His will and His works.
His holiness is the basis of all of His other attributes.
His perfection is celebrated before the Throne of
Heaven—the seraphim crying, "Holy, Holy, Holy is the
Lord of Host." (Isaiah 6:3)

God swears by His "holiness" because that is a fuller
expression of Himself than anything else. (Psalm 89:35)

Love

Love is patient, love is kind. It does not envy, it does not boast, it is not proud. It is not rude, it is not self-seeking, it is not easily angered, it keeps no record of wrongs. Love does not delight in evil but rejoices with the truth. It always protects, always trusts, always hopes, always perseveres. And now these three remain; faith, hope and love. But the greatest of these is love.

I Corinthians 13: 4-7, 13)

Faith is the foundation and content of God's message; hope is the attitude and focus; love is the action. Love shows unselfish service to others, the evidence that we care.

Love in Action

Positive	Negative
Love is patient	Does not envy
Love is kind	Does not boast
Always protects	Is not proud
Always trusts	Is not rude
Always hopes	Is not self-seeking
Always perseveres	Is not easily angered
Rejoices with truth	Keeps no record of
wrongs	
Love never fails	Does not delight in evil

Prayer

For this reason I bow my knees to the Father of our Lord Jesus Christ --- that He would grant you, according to the riches of His glory, to be strengthened with might through His Spirit in the inner man.
Ephesians 3: 14, 16 KJV

This could be my personal prayer and a prayer of intercession on behalf of others.

Spiritually—I am confused so I pray for understanding.

Jesus prayed for His disciples: "Sanctify them by your truth." (John 17:17)

Physically—I am tired so I pray for rest. In God's care I find rest and security. (Psalm 16:8-9)

Emotionally—I am very weak, so I pray for strength. You give hope and relief from distress. (Psalm 4:1; 107-6)

Mentally—I am worried so I pray for peace. You promise insight and wisdom when I cry out to you. (Proverbs 2:3-6; James 1:5-7)

I will turn my cares into prayers.

What a friend we have in Jesus,
All our sins and griefs to bear!
What a privilege to carry
Every thing to God in prayer!
Scriven

March 4

Children

*Lo, children are an heritage of the Lord: and the fruit of
the womb is his reward. Psalm 127:3*

When we consider children, in our society today,
we need to see them through the eyes of Jesus—a
blessing from God. Many are unwanted and others are
mistreated. How can we expect God to bless our nation
while we ignore His heritage and His reward?

Every child needs parents who love God and recognize
their dependence upon Him. Parents who teach and
live as an example of faith and trust in God. Parents
who pray for, and with their children, teaching them of
God's love and faithfulness.

It has been said that Susannah Wesley (mother of John
and Charles Wesley) spent one hour praying each day
for her 17 children.

Some rules she followed in training her children:

1. Subdue self will in a child and work together with
   God.
2. Teach him to pray as soon as he can speak.
3. Give him nothing he cries for and only what is good
   for him if he asks politely.
4. To prevent lying, punish no fault that is freely
   confessed but never allow a rebellious sinful act to
   go unchecked.
5. Command and reward good behavior.
6. Strictly observe all promises you have made to your
   children.

Christian Living

For you were once darkness, but now you are light in the
Lord. Live as children of light, (for the fruit of the light
consist in all goodness, righteousness, and truth) and
find out what pleases the Lord.
Ephesians 5: 8-10

What does it mean to live as "children of light?" Find
out what pleases the Lord and live to please Him. It's
not whether I like it or not, nor whether other people
approve or disapprove!

The letters WWJD has been popular among Christians
over the past few years. <u>W</u>hat <u>W</u>ould <u>J</u>esus <u>D</u>o? As we
ask ourselves this question we need to consider three
things:

> Is it good?
> Is it right?
> Is it true?

Jesus always did what pleased the Father and this is
His desire for us.

"He has shown you, O man, what is good. And what
does the Lord require of you? To act justly and to love
mercy and to walk humbly with your God." (Micah
6:8)

Prepared for Battle

Finally, be strong in the Lord and in his mighty power.
Put on the whole armor of God so that you can take your
stand against the devil's schemes.
Ephesians 6:10-11

Satan is alive and well but he is a defeated foe   Christ won the victory over Satan when He died on the cross, came forth from the grave and ascended back to heaven where He is with the Father today. He paid the penalty for sin and gave me life eternal. I am in Him and He is in me. (John 14:20) By his power in me I can resist Satan and he has no choice but to flee. (James 4:7)

I can stand in the mighty power of Jesus, dressed in the armor of God:

The Belt of Truth—Jesus is Truth. I am in Him,
He is in me.

The Breastplate of Righteousness—I stand in
Christ's righteousness.

The Sandals of Peace—I have peace with God in Christ.

I take up the Shield of Faith—In the victory of Christ.

Put on the Helmet of Salvation—To protect my mind.

Use the Sword of the Spirit—The Word of God.

These will ensure my success in battle.

March 7

Death

Even though I walk through the valley of the shadow of death, I will fear no evil, for you are with me; your rod and your staff, they comfort me.

Psalm 23:4

When speaking of death, I sometimes say, "I don't fear death but I fear the process of dying." The process may involve pain, suffering, disease or injury, but not always, so I must trust God to make the choice because He knows best. I have His promise—"Never will I leave you; never will I forsake you." (Hebrews 13:5)

Your rod and your staff, they comfort me. God's rod is a symbol of His power and authority. His staff is a symbol of protection and security. His sustaining grace is sufficient in my weakness (II Corinthians 12:9), therefore I can lean upon His power, His provision, and His protection when I walk through the valley of the "shadow of death," into eternity with Christ.

Fear or faith, which shall it be?
Christ won the victory on Calvary!
I am in Christ and He is in me;
He conquered death for Eternity!

March 8

Children

*Train a child in the way he should go, and when he is
old he will not turn from it.*
Proverbs 22:6

How should he go? It is natural to want to bring up our
children alike; or train them the same way—the way we
want them to go. This verse involves more than we may
have considered. It implies that parents should discern
the individuality, special abilities and strengths that
God has given each one. We are all unique individuals.

It's true, that we should teach our children about God
and their relationship with Him, but it is vital that
training goes along with the teaching. This is the
area in which we, as parents, often fail and cannot
understand why our children may turn from what we
thought they were taught.

To teach is to impart knowledge. To train is to instruct,
encourage and discipline. Training is much harder
than teaching. It takes time, love and understanding.
This is what Paul is talking about in Ephesians 6:4.

Only through God's grace and patience can we be the
parents He has called us to be.

March 9

Prayer

And pray in the Spirit on all occasions with all kinds of prayers and requests. With this in mind, be alert and always keep on praying for all the saints.
Ephesians 6:18

Prayer is a special privilege that we have as a child of God. Our God is a personal God who delights to have fellowship with His children. He longs to reveal Himself in a personal way as we realize more and more our dependence upon Him.

Praying "in the Spirit" means according to the Spirit's leading, allowing the Holy Spirit to pray through us because He knows the mind of the Father—what God wants to do and how He wants to do it. (Romans 8:27)

On all occasions means "in every situation," good or bad, with prayers of praise, thanksgiving, intercession, petition, confession and repentance. Our prayers are to include all of God's family, those we know and the church around the world.

God's will for us is to pray, pray, pray! (I Thessalonians 5:17-18)

March 10

Temptation

These things happened to them as examples and were written down as warnings for us, on whom the fulfillment of the ages has come. So, if you think you are standing firm, be careful that you don't fall!

I Corinthians 20:11-12

The things Paul is talking about is what happened when God was leading Israel from Egypt to the Promised Land. He tells us what Israel did and the consequences of their attitude and actions. We are to heed them as warnings and not fall as they did.

It has been said, "A wise man learns from another man's mistakes, a fool learns from his own." The Bible records the sins of many individuals and the consequences they experienced. We need to study God's Word so we can know His will and ways for us. It is not a question of "if" we are tempted, but "when" we are tempted, because all of us will be tempted at some time.

The source of temptation is:
The world—a drawing to its sensual lifestyle
The flesh—desire to be in control
The devil—seeks to turn us from God

God never tempts us but may test us to reveal, to us, what our motives and attitudes are. (James 1:19)

Our most vulnerable times are during illness, pride, weariness, lust or anger. God is faithful to provide a way out. (I Corinthians 10:13). Call on Him!

Temptation: The thought or desire to act in opposition to God's Word.

March 11

Our Nation

Blessed is the Nation whose God is the Lord, the people
he chose for his inheritance.
Psalm 33:12

God has truly blessed our Nation. This country was founded on biblical principles and a Christ-centered interpretation of justice, fairness and equal opportunity. We have taken for granted our blessings and forgotten our Godly heritage even to denying the Sovereign God who chose to bless us.

Our forefathers suffered and struggled to establish a nation where they were free to worship the Living Eternal Personal God and serve Him as Lord of their lives.

As a result of our freedom we have become a selfish, immoral, prideful nation, who has forgotten how to be thankful. We need to seek God's face in confession and repentance and cry out the words of Irving Berlin's song, "God Bless America." Maybe God will hear and restore us to our first love.

> God bless America, land that I love.
> Stand beside her and guide her
> Through the night with a light from above.
> From the mountains to the prairies,
> To the ocean white with foam;
> God bless America, my home sweet home.

March 12

Spiritual Growth

*Like newborn babies, crave pure spiritual milk, so that
by it you may grow up in your salvation.*
I Peter 2:2

The desire to grow up physically is natural. Children
want to become like their older siblings or their parents.
They observe behavior, walk and talk of others and
make the application in their life.

Peter compares the spiritual life of the newborn
Christian with physical birth. First, we are to crave
spiritual "milk" of the Word then move to "solid
food" of the Word to grow up and become mature. (I
Corinthians 3:2; Hebrews 5:12-14)

God's desire for His children is for them to grow
spiritually, becoming more like Christ. (Romans 8:29)
The way we can grow is through His Word - studying
and obeying His principles.

Once we see our need for God's Word and begin to
find nourishment in Christ, our spiritual appetite will
increase, and we will start to mature. As we focus
more on our spiritual growth we will find peace and
fulfillment in pleasing the Lord.

Prayer—Faith

But as for me, I watch in hope for the Lord, I wait for
God my Savior; my God will hear me.

Micah 7:7

Do I express faith and confidence, when I pray, as Micah did? Sometimes; but not always. I have no cause to doubt God's faithfulness but my faith is sometimes weak because I have neglected my fellowship with God.

My relationship with God must be nurtured day by day if I am to know Him as he is—a loving, caring, faithful Father.

> Little faith—believes God can do.
> Great faith—believes God will do.
> Perfect faith—believes God has done.

My faith is expressed when I willingly act on that faith in a positive way. My God will hear me!

"Call to me and I will answer you and tell you great and unsearchable things you do not know." (Jeremiah 33:3)

March 14

Faith

Though the fig tree does not bud and there are no grapes on the vines, though the olive crop fails and the fields produce no food, though there are no sheep in the pen and no cattle in the stalls, yet I will rejoice in the Lord, I will be joyful in God my Savior.

Habakkuk 3:17-18

Habakkuk's faith was not controlled by the events around him but by his faith in God to provide. His eyes were on God, not circumstances.

Are you able to praise God before the answer comes? The praise for past blessings is sweet to God's ears but much sweeter is the praise from a thankful heart that knows all will be well.

This is "perfect faith!"

"Jehovah Jireh." God will provide.

I will trust while I wait,
For my God is never late.

March 15

Temptation

Watch and pray so that you will not fall into temptation.
The Spirit is willing but the body is weak.

Matthew 26:41

Jesus' words to Peter were a warning that is as relative today as it was when He spoke them. We are faced with temptation every day, therefore we need to watch and pray. To watch means being aware of the possibilities of temptation; sensitive to the subtle ways of Satan. Praying prepares us spiritually to fight it (or resist it). Only in God's strength can we defeat Satan's power.

We cannot keep the temptations from coming but we can choose how we will respond. God's Spirit in our spirit will enable us to resist when we pray. If we choose to yield then Satan has won the battle.

We are in a "spiritual battle" every day. We must put on the armor but we must also watch and pray. (Ephesians 6:18)

March 16

Forgiveness

*Be kind and compassionate to one another, forgiving
each other, just as in Christ God forgave you.*
Ephesians 4:32

More than once Christ emphasized the principle of
forgiveness. He reminded us, in His model prayer, how
important the practice of a forgiving spirit is in the life
of a Christian.

A "root of bitterness" can spring up in the unforgiving
heart and as a result our attitudes and actions are filtered
through that root. It will affect our relationships; and
our fellowship with God.

A bitter root comes when we allow disappointment to
grow into resentment or when we nurse grudges over
past hurts. Forgiveness doesn't mean forgetting what
happened or pretending it never occurred. It means a
deliberate action of the will on our part. We release the
offender from any obligation on our part. It is an act of
mercy just as God has done toward us.

March 17

Rebellion

But the people refused to listen to Samuel. No! they said.
We want a king over us. Then we will be like all the
other nations with a king to lead us and go out before us
and fight our battles.
I Samuel 8:19-20

God's purpose for the Nation of Israel was to make Himself known to the other nations. As their God, He would use them to demonstrate His power, to protect and provide for their needs, as they trusted Him. His desire was that other nations would turn to Him as they saw what He did for Israel.

God was their King but they rejected Him because they wanted to be like other nations—like everybody else, the world. God allowed them to have what they wanted—an earthly king—but they could no longer fulfill the purpose for which they were called, so God has set them aside for a period of time.

Christ is building His Church today to make God known to the world and to carry on the ministry He began while on earth. Christ is the Head and the Church is His body, dependent upon Him, a called out people to be different from the world.

When God's people want to be like unbelievers, they are heading for spiritual disaster.

March 18

Wisdom

*If any of you lacks wisdom, he should ask God, who
gives generously to all without finding fault, and it will
be given to him.*
James 1:5

James is not thinking so much about knowledge, but
the ability to make decisions in difficult circumstances.
As a Christian, I don't have to grope around trying to
find an answer, but I can ask God for wisdom to make
the right choice.

How often do you pray for wisdom? We should not wait
until some big decision is necessary. It should be our
daily prayer for the small decisions in life because the
small decisions lead to the big choices. Wisdom means
practical discernment to know right from wrong.

God does not grant requests that would hurt us or
others or that would violate His own nature or will. We
must believe God's way is best and be willing to obey
Him. We should ask God for wisdom to know what to
do and for courage to follow through.

When I'm going through trials I need God's wisdom to
know—Is it from God or Satan? Testing or tempting?
To strengthen my faith, to teach me truth or to correct
through discipline.

Testimony

Even when I am old and ray, do not forsake me, O Lord
(God) till I declare your power to the next generation,
your might to all who are to come.

Psalm 71:18

What is a testimony? We usually think of it as what happened in our initial experience of salvation. That is a part of it, but it involves more. God continues working in our lives daily to conform us to the image of Christ. How we respond to Him will determine the record of our testimony.

Our testimony relates to our character, our conduct and our conversation.

Our character should display a spirit of obedience. An obedient spirit follows the Lord's guidance, no matter what the circumstances are. What we tell others should line up with what God sees in our heart. We are to be holy even as God is holy.

Our conduct, or what we do, is another facet of our testimony. We've heard the saying, "actions speak louder than words." If what we say conflicts with our behavior, then we cloud our witness. The way we act should confirm who we are in Christ.

Our conversation should reveal what Christ is doing in our lives and what He wants to do in each individual life (person). As we share His Word and His work it can make the difference between doubt and faith in another person's life.

March 20

Faith

*In the same way, faith by itself, if it is not accompanied
by action, is dead.*
James 2:17

I'm sure you have heard the expression, "put your money where your mouth is," or "back up your word with actions." That's what James is saying in this verse. Someone has said, "Talk is cheap." James says it's dead without deeds.

There is a process that shapes our beliefs which can also turn a hint of faith into action. It begins in the mind. We think about the issue, what the need is and consider the possible solution. We talk to God about it, and discuss it with someone we trust and we may gain some new insights. Maybe we become more aware of what is involved. Then we realize we must do something. We're faced with a decision—to act on faith and know what God will do or waver in our faith and always wonder, "what if."

> You are God Almighty,
> All things are possible with you.
> I am in Christ and Christ is in me;
> Your grace is sufficient to see me through.

March 21

Prayer

Have faith in God, Jesus answered. Therefore I tell you,
whatever you ask for in prayer, believe that you have
received it, and it will be yours.

Mark 11:22-24

Sometimes we have a problem with this verse when we pray. We tell ourselves that Jesus didn't really mean it like He said it. Jesus is the Truth. Why should we doubt what He said? We question whether God will do what we ask. Jesus went beyond that and said we are to believe we have already received, not maybe, but it's done so we are to thank Him.

All Christians have been given a measure of faith. How we exercise that faith is our choice and it will determine how God is able to use us for His glory.

A pouring out of the deepest and truest feelings, a communication of spirit with Spirit; that is what praying is about.

March 22

The Name of Jesus

Therefore God exalted Him to the highest place and gave him the name that is above every name, that at the name of Jesus every knee should bow, in heaven and on earth, and every tongue confess that Jesus Christ is Lord, to the glory of God the Father.
Philippians 2:9-11

The world needs to take note of who Jesus is. He is above all—in heaven, on earth and under the earth.

"The name of God in the Old Testament denotes the divine Presence, the divine majesty, especially as the object of adoration and praise." (Wuest's Word Studies). The authority that Jesus Christ exercised over nature and the spirit world is an expression of His divine nature. He is God in flesh. When He speaks all creation obeys.

"The name of the Lord is a strong tower; the righteous run to it and are safe." (Proverbs 18:10)

Jesus has given His followers the privilege of speaking "in His name," but we must understand what that involves. It is more than a casual phrase at the end of a prayer. Our will must be in submission to His will, according to His will and nature. He must be glorified. It's all about Him—not us.

March 23

God's Sovereignty

Call upon me in the day of trouble; I shall rescue you,
and you will honor Me.
Psalm 50:15 NASB

God is good and He is in control but that does not prevent bad things from happening. If we never experience bad in our lives we can never know how good God is. God is able to reveal Himself to us, who He really is, as He ministers to us in trying circumstances.

God is Sovereign over everything. He can stop sin or He can allow it to run its full course and work it's consequences into His plan for our lives. He allows us to choose how we will respond to each situation in our life.

The wisest plan is to obey God so He can work His perfect will for us. He is faithful to his promises. However, when we choose otherwise and He allows His permissive will, He is still faithful when we are ready to confess and repent. (I John 1:9)

March 24

Beatitudes

Blessed are those who are persecuted because of righteousness, for theirs is the kingdom of heaven.
Matthew 5:10

God is in control and only as we trust in Him can we be freed from fear of our enemies. When He rules our thoughts and emotions we cannot be shaken by anything our enemies can do.

Jesus goes on to say, "Rejoice and be glad, for great is your reward in heaven."

These sayings of Jesus are referred to as The Beatitudes—not do attitudes—but attitudes that characterize the Christian life. We are sometimes so focused on doing that we forget to be what God called us to be—conformed to the image of Christ. What He called us to be He will enable us to become.

One of the most visible changes in the life of a new Christian is the change in attitudes. We begin to see people and problems from God's perspective.

The word, "Blessed" goes beyond happiness—it means the experience of hope and joy, independent of outward circumstances. It comes through following Jesus.

March 25

Prayer

The effective prayer of a righteous man can accomplish much.
James 5:16b

The Lord hears and will respond to the petitions of the righteous. The Greek word of "accomplish" is the one from which we get our English word for energy. James is saying that in response to the effective prayer of a believer, God directs His supernatural energy toward the crisis. However, there are no prayer formulas or perfect words that cause Him to act.

The Lord responds to faith so the godly believer will see Him intervene. The bible refers to two kinds of righteousness—positional, in which all believers stand before God, in Christ. Then there is practical (progressive) righteousness, which we walk with a clear conscience of obedience in our daily lives.

Psalm 66:18 says, "If I regard wickedness in my heart, the Lord will not hear." We must repent of all known sin before we can expect God to act. God wants to intervene on our behalf. His love demands that He comfort, strengthen and help us when we are troubled. We clear the way for Him to respond when we keep a clear conscience.

Prayer

And I will do whatever you ask me in my name, so that
the Son may bring glory to the Father. You may ask me
for anything in my name, and I will do it.

John 14: 13-14

Some people take this as an unlimited promise—"name it and claim it," but what Jesus is saying here goes far beyond that. Much of Jesus' teaching while on earth concerned prayer. We need to consider all of these and especially His personal prayers.

There are three things he always focused on: Believe (have faith), pray in His name, for God's glory. If we are sincerely following God and seeking His will, then our request will be in line with what He wants and He will grant it. If we are earnestly desiring to please Him, we will pray with an open heart and mind, willing to adjust our plans to His.

As we learn to trust Him for answers according to His will and time frame, He gives us greater tasks in prayer. He wants us involved in His work. He is pleased when we ask Him to meet our needs or the needs of someone else. Pray and believe; you will receive!

The Spirit

*So I say live by the Spirit, and you will not gratify the
desires of the sinful nature. Since we live by the Spirit,
let us keep in step with the Spirit.*
Galatians 5: 16, 25

Being led by the Spirit involves the desire to hear, the
readiness to obey and the sensitivity to discern between
my feelings and God's promptings.

When I allow myself to be controlled and guided by the
Holy Spirit, the words of Christ will be in my mind, the
love of Christ will be behind my actions, and the power
of Christ will help me control my selfish desires.

If I rely on my own wisdom I will make wrong choices.
When I try to follow the Spirit in my own effort I fail. I
must allow the Holy Spirit to empower me.

He fruit of the Spirit is the spontaneous work of the
Holy Spirit in our lives.

Peace

Let the peace of Christ rule in your hearts, since as members of one body you were called to peace, and be thankful.
Colossians 3:15

Christians should live in peace. We have peace with God and we can have the peace of God as we obey Him and live by His principles. It doesn't mean that we are to think alike but that we can work together despite our differences. The love we are to express is not a feeling but a decision to be concerned for one another.

Our hearts are the center of conflict because our feelings and desires clash and there is a constant struggle to live as God wants us to live.

The mind is the control tower of life. Decisions determine actions which in turn affect the immediate and distant future. What we think today will determine what we do tomorrow. If we are to walk pleasing to the Lord, then we must program our mind with godly thinking.

How? By sifting our thoughts through God's Word and will. When a thought is unscriptural we must reject it. (II Corinthians 10:5) Scripture is the instruction manual for our control tower.

Conscience

*Holding on to faith and a good conscience. Some have
rejected these and so have shipwrecked their faith.*
I Timothy 1:19

How can you hold on to a good conscience? Treasure
your faith in Christ more than anything else and do
what you know is right.

Many people mistakenly see their conscience as God's
voice instead of God's gift. We were created with an
"inner monitor," that acts as a moral compass for life;
it points to a standard of right and wrong that can
guide our decisions and actions. But the conscience,
like everything else has fallen to sin. It must be
programmed to godly thinking of right and wrong or it
can nudge us in the wrong direction.

We can let our conscience be our guide only through
the transforming power of the Holy Spirit.

Paul was being led by his conscience when he was killing
Christians. He thought he was doing God a favor.

By understanding our conscience as a divine gift, we
stand a better chance of staying out of trouble.

Eternal Life

Now this is eternal life; that they may know you, the only true God, and Jesus Christ, whom you have sent.
John 17:3

Eternal life—what does it mean and how do we get it? Eternal has to do with eternity—no end. It is God's gift to us when we know Him in a personal way through Jesus Christ, His son, whom He sent to earth as the Savior of mankind. Eternal life is life that never ends.

Eternal life involves more than the quantity of time (everlasting life), without end. Eternal life, in Christ, also involves a quality of life, a special relationship with God the Father, God the Son and God the Holy Spirit. We can know God as He has revealed Himself through Jesus Christ, who is the Living Word of God, recorded in the written Word of God—the Bible.

We experience Eternal life when we exercise faith in God's promise of salvation to those who believe in Jesus as Lord and Savior. (John 3:16)

Testing

Consider it pure joy, my brothers, whenever you face trials of many kinds, because you know that the testing of your faith develops perseverance.
James 1:2-3

James doesn't say, "If you face trials," but "when you face trials." Trials are evident in life. God allows Christians to experience trials and testing. He has a purpose for them and He will see us through them.

1) He sometimes will use painful experiences to cleanse and purify our lives. As we turn to the Lord at these times we are able to see from His perspective and are more aware of our sins.

2) Sometimes He allows difficulty as a way of testing us—trying our faith and endurance or devotion to Him. These times can strengthen our faith and develop us spiritually.

3) God uses suffering to demonstrate His power to sustain us. He is glorified as He brings us through these experiences and others see His working in our lives. They are encouraged in their trials.

As we evaluate these experiences in our lives we can see how God's providential hand carried us through.

April

April 1

Holy Spirit

When he comes (the Holy Spirit), he will convict the world of guilt in regard to sin and righteousness and judgment: in regard to sin because men do not believe in me, in regard to righteousness, because I'm going to the Father, where you can see me no longer; and, in regard to judgment, because the prince of this world now stands condemned. John 16:8-11

The Holy Spirit is our divine helper and instructor. He guides the believer into all truth, revealing God's thoughts and purposes for our lives. He accomplishes this in three ways:

Evangelism—pointing out how our sin separates us from God and how the death and life of Christ brings us to salvation.

Discipleship—teaching us how to walk in obedience to God's Word and relate to one another.

Missionary—directs us in sharing our faith through our character and conduct.

Jesus would no longer be in the world physically to call people to repentance nor to reveal the standard of God's righteousness to anyone who believes, nor to demonstrate His power over Satan. The Holy Spirit would accomplish His work through His Spiritual Body—the Church.

The Holy Spirit also told the disciples "what is to come" and they wrote it down in the books that form our New Testament.

April 2

One Way

For there is one God and one mediator between God and man, the man Christ Jesus, who gave himself as a ransom for all men.

I Timothy 2:5-6

Christianity has been referred to as an exclusive religion because of the teaching that Jesus Christ is the only way to God. Paul makes it very clear, in his letter to Timothy, that there is no other way. Jesus, Himself, said, "I am the way, the truth and the life, no man comes to the Father except by me."

The problem is not Christianity and Jesus as the only way to God. The problem is with God and His Word - doubt that God's Word is Truth. Eve was deceived by Satan and led to doubt God's Word and man has continued to fall for Satan's deception.

We must choose to believe the Bible is God's Word or reject it as truth. If we reject His written Word we also reject His Living Word, the Lord Jesus Christ. To doubt God's Word is to doubt God, for His word is the revelation of Himself.

"In the beginning was the Word, and the Word was with God and the Word was God. (John 1:1)

April 3

Assurance

And this is the testimony: God has given us eternal life,
and this life is in His Son. He who has the Son has life;
he who does not have the Son of God does not have life.

I John 5:11-12

Eternal life is a gift from God, through His Son, the
Lord Jesus Christ. Whoever believes in God's Son has
eternal life. You don't need to wait for eternal life,
because it begins the moment you believe. You don't
need to work for it because it is already yours. You
don't need to worry about it because it comes from God
and it is guaranteed.

Three things that can cause doubt:

1) Unconfessed sin. Satan tempts us to sin and when
   we yield he condemns us - accuses - until we
   confess and claim God's promise. (I John 1:9)

2) Ignorance of God's Word. If a believer is not well
   grounded scripturally, he can be fooled by false
   teaching such as—can't be sure or can lose our
   salvation. We must study the Word.

3) Reliance on emotions. Eternal life is based on
   facts not feelings. Our certainty is based on God's
   promise that He has given us life through His Son.
   This is true whether you feel close to God or far
   way.

Get to know Satan's subtle ways and reject him in the
name of Jesus.

April 4

New Life

Therefore if anyone is in Christ, he is a new creation; the old has gone, the new has come!
II Corinthians 5:17

Because Christ died, in our place, to pay the penalty for sin, we are dead to our old life. Christ's death on Calvary bought every person a life free from the wages of sin, but each individual must accept that gift of salvation for him or herself. No sin is so great that God will not forgive when we confess and repent.

Christians are brand new people on the inside. The Holy Spirit gives them new life, and they are not the same any more. We are not reformed, rehabilitated, or reeducated—we are recreated living in union with Christ. (Colossians 2:6-7)

We are not merely turning over a new leaf; we are beginning a new life under a new Master.

John Newton wrote the song entitled, "Amazing Grace," as his testimony of what happened in his experience of salvation.

Every believer can give testimony to the same experience.

April 5

All-knowing God

And you, my son Solomon, acknowledge the God of your father, and serve him with whole hearted devotion and with a willing mind, for the Lord searches every heart and understands every motive behind the thoughts ---

I Chronicles 28:9a

Nothing can be hidden from God. He knows our inner most thoughts and intentions. This should be comforting to our hearts because God knows the worst about us but he loves us still. Knowing this we should desire to walk in His ways.

We rejoice when God answers prayer and are amazed when he reveals a new scriptural truth. Yet, we are slow in recognizing His working in the minor details of our daily life.

At the moment of salvation we are given an amazing gift—the Holy Spirit, who provides spiritual discernment. He helps us to understand God's working to conform us to the image of Christ.

The Lord wants us to see what He is doing so our faith will be strengthened.

April 6

God Speaks

*This is what the Almighty says, In a little while I will
once more shake the heavens and the earth, the sea and
the dry land.*

Haggai 2:6

We need ears to hear when God speaks. He is not limited
in the ways He seeks to get our attention. He speaks
through His creation—nature, people, circumstances—
and, through His Holy Spirit.

The Words, "in a little while," are not limited to a
particular historical context but they refer to God's
control—He can act whenever He chooses. He is not
bound by time. Time was created for man by God.

Throughout God's Word, reference is made to ways
He used the wind, clouds, sun, lightning, earthquakes,
floods, and famines to declare warnings of judgment.

"See to it that you do not refuse him who speaks. If
they did not escape when they refused him who warned
them on earth, how much less will we, if we turn away
from him who warns us from heaven? (Hebrews 12:25)

God's judgment is coming—we need to heed His
warnings and turn to Him in repentance.

April 7

Faith

But he said to me, My grace is sufficient for you, for my power is made perfect in weakness. Therefore I will boast more gladly about my weaknesses, so that Christ's power may rest on me.

II Corinthians 12:9

My faith is not weak when I am weak because I will recognize my own helplessness and seek God's help. Then my faith becomes strong in Him as Christ takes over.

When I am strong in my own power and ability, my faith is weak and ineffective. God allows me to do what I can do which results in nothing "worthwhile."

It is through troubles and trials that my faith increases, as I depend upon God's grace through the power of the Holy Spirit.

April 8

Trials

Consider it pure joy, brothers, whenever you face trials of many kinds, because you know that the testing of your faith develops perseverance. Perseverance must finish its work so that you may be mature and complete, not lacking anything.

James 1:2-4

James doesn't say "be happy" when trials come, but to "consider it joy." It is not what happens outside but what is going on inside—how I respond to what God wants to do in my life.

If I never hurt, how can I know God as the Comforter or Healer? If I never struggled how can I know Him as my Helper? God reveals Himself to us through our storms in life. If we are not tested we cannot be victorious. As we trust God, He brings us through each difficulty and enables us to encourage someone else.

April 9

Daily Living

*Since, then, you have been raised with Christ, set your
hearts on things above, where Christ is seated at the
right hand of God. Set your minds on things above, not
on earthly things.*

Colossians 3:1-2

I am in Christ and Christ is in me. When He was
resurrected I was raised in Him. Someone has said,
"I'm just a poor sinner in this world trying to get to
heaven." This is not true. I'm a citizen of heaven
trying to get through this World.

The best way to get through this world is to set my
heart and mind on Christ who is in heaven at the right
hand of God. This means focusing on the eternal
rather than the temporal—looking at life from God's
perspective and to seek what He desires. The more I
regard the world around me as God does, the more I
can live in harmony with Him.

Paul goes on to say, in verse 2, "and your life is hidden
with Christ, in God." Hidden means safe and secure
with Christ in Glory."

If we keep our hearts in the next world it will be easier
to keep our heads in this one.

April 10

Salvation

Whoever believes in the Son has eternal life, but whoever rejects the Son will not see life, for God's wrath remains on him.

John 3:36

If we focus on God's love but fail to understand His wrath we cannot see the significance of Christ's death, burial and resurrection. The world believes that all will be saved because God loves us. "God is love," (I John 4:16), but it's not His love that saves us—it's the death of Jesus, His Son, as our substitute in death. God's wrath against sin demanded the penalty for sin (death) to be paid.

Because of God's grace (His goodness toward us) He provided His Son to die in our place. When we accept Jesus as our substitute—by faith—then we have eternal life.

Those who reject Christ, reject God's provision for salvation and eternal life.

Jesus answered, "I am the way, and the truth and the life. No one comes to the Father except through me." (John 14:6)

God's love cannot save us—only the death of His Son and faith in Him.

April 11

Prayer

Be joyful in hope, patient in affliction, faithful in prayer.
Romans 12:12

When we are serious about prayer our intimacy with Christ will grow. We come to know God better as we speak and listen to Him. We begin to view the world from His perspective. His concerns will become our concerns.

As we study the Scriptures the Holy Spirit will work God's truth deep into our hearts. Consistent exposure to His Word will reveal ungodliness in our lives and the Spirit will give us power to change.

Through prayer we will receive peace, joy and direction even when circumstances don't change. Then we are able to be joyful in hope and patient in affliction.

The secret of power in prayer is knowing the Word of God and the God of the Word.

April 12

Armor of God—Spiritual Battle

Therefore, put on the full armor of God, so that when the day of evil comes, you may be able to stand your ground.
Ephesians 6:13

Notice that Paul doesn't say, "if" the day of evil comes, but "when" it comes. We can be assured it will come. He doesn't say flee or fight, he says, "stand." Not in our own strength but in the Lord's mighty power. Four times in this passage Paul reminds us to "stand."

God has provided armor to protect us. When we received Christ we also received "the belt of truth," for Christ is Truth. We received the "breastplate of righteousness," for Christ is our righteousness. We received the "sandals of peace," for Christ is our peace.

In addition to these we are to "take up," (they are available but must be appropriated) the "shield of faith," the "helmet of salvation," the sword of the "Spirit," (the Word) and the "privilege of prayer," (the power of the Holy Spirit).

We are in Christ and Christ is in us. He is our victory!

April 13

Faithfulness

*We continually remember before our God and Father,
your work produced by faith, your labor prompted by
love, and your endurance inspired by hope in our Lord
Jesus Christ.*

I Thessalonians 1:3

These characteristics are the marks of an effective
Christian.

Our faith in Christ enables us to serve Him in
the power of the Holy Spirit. Our love for Christ
encourages us to do our best and our hope in Him
inspires us to press on for God's glory.

Faith is the foundation and content of God's message.
Hope is the attitude and focus.
Love is the action.

When faith and hope are in line we can freely express
our love to God and His love will be shed abroad in
our heart.

*"And now these three remain: faith, hope and love.
But the greatest of these is love." I Corinthians 13:13*

April 14

Prayer

*This is the confidence we have in approaching God: that
if we ask anything according to his will, he hears us.
And if we know that he hear us—whatever we ask—we
know that we have what we asked of him.*

I John 5:14-15 NIV

The Father always keeps His promises. How can we claim His promises? The emphasis here is on God's will, not our will. The main focus of our prayer is to know God's will and then ask that He grant it for His glory.

We need to become familiar with the promises in His Word. Some are limited to a certain situation (Genesis 17:16). Many promises are meant for all believers, for example: God's assurance that He will never leave us. (Hebrews 13:5)

Some promises are conditional. Example: the guarantee of Psalm 37:4 requires obedience. "Delight yourself in the Lord and He will give you the desires of your heart."

Our attitude, motive and actions are important when we consider God's will, as well as our desire or request. Does it contradict the Word of God? Will it contribute to my spiritual growth? Does the Holy Spirit witness to my spirit that my request pleases God?

April 15

Power of God

Jesus replied, What is impossible with men is possible with God.
Luke 18:27 NIV

We serve a God of the impossible—He can make a way where there is no way.

We have become a generation of self-sufficiency, focused on what we are able to accomplish through our own power, promotion and performance. What we do not realize is our failure in the important things—life, death, relationships, health, happiness—things outside our control.

I remember when my children were very small, trying to accomplish a task, I would offer my help and immediately they would say, "I can do it myself." Human nature does not want to be dependent in any situation. We become frustrated when we can't "do on our own."

When we are willing to acknowledge our dependence on God, our Creator, we will experience the joy of seeing what He can do for us, in us and through us. We will experience the impossible.

April 16

God's Faithfulness

*Being confident of this, that he who began a good work
in you will carry it on to completion until the day of
Christ Jesus.*

Philippians 1:6 NIV

Sometimes we feel that God is far away from us and we
may wonder if He is really personally involved in our
lives. Psalm 139 tells us how intimately involved God
is in our lives. He loves us unconditionally—not based
on what we do or fail to do—but because His nature is
love.

God who began a good work in us will continue it
throughout our lifetime and will finish it when we meet
Him face to face. God's work for us began when Christ
died on the cross in our place. His work in us began
when we accepted Christ as Lord. Now the Holy Spirit
lives in us, enabling us to be more like Christ.

There may be times when we feel that we are not
making any progress in our spiritual life. When
you feel incomplete, unfinished, or distressed by
your shortcomings, remember God's promises and
provisions. God won't give up on you.

Don't let your present condition rob you of the joy of
knowing Christ, or keep you from growing closer to
Him.

April 17

Prayer

In that day you will no longer ask me anything. I tell you the truth, my Father will give you whatever you ask in my name.

John 16:23 NIV

What day is Jesus referring to? Jesus was preparing His disciples for His return to the Father in heaven. He would no longer be physically present for them to ask Him anything but He wanted them to know that now they had a new relationship with God. Because of His resurrection they could approach the Father in His name and the Father would give them what they asked.

Before Christ's death and resurrection it was necessary to go through a priest to approach God. Now we approach Him through Jesus, our Great High Priest.

When we approach God we need to remember three things if we expect Him to answer our prayers:

> No unconfessed sin in our life.
> Faith in God's Word.
> The power of Jesus' Name.

When we pray in this way the Father will hear and answer our prayer.

April 18

Anger

In your anger do not sin: Do not let the sun go down while you are still angry, and do not give the devil a foothold.
Ephesians 4:26-27

Have you considered the connection between Satan and anger? We think of anger in relation to self or someone else, never realizing how Satan can use it as a prime tool in his deceptive way. He is so subtle in the way he builds a stronghold that controls our thoughts and actions.

We are not told that we should never feel angry but we are told how to handle our anger in a proper way. Paul says, "In your anger do not sin." How do I deal with it?

1) Admit I am angry
2) Why and with whom am I upset
3) Deal with it through forgiveness (of myself or another)

If we allow anger to control us it can damage relationships and also cause inner turmoil— mental, emotional, spiritual and physical.

The Holy Spirit will enable us to overcome the temptations we face day by day, when we admit our dependence on Him.

April 19

The Word

*Do not merely listen to the Word, and so deceive
yourselves. Do what it says.*

James 1:22

What place does God's Word have in your life? Why do
you read it? Because of a sense of guilt or do you really
want to know the truth? The only source of truth
is Scripture. Living by Biblical principles protects
believers from Satan's deception. Knowing God's
Word helps us to discern truth from error as the Holy
Spirit brings the Word to our mind.

We can build truth into our life as we obey God's Word.
The Holy Spirit provides the construction material but
we have to put it together as He gives wisdom and
guidance.

As we have a need we can turn to a concordance for
verses related to the topic we're studying. As we study
those verses it can give us a blueprint to follow in
meeting our need. As we follow the leading of the Holy
Spirit He will continue filling our mind with truth and
enable us to live by God's principles through divine
power. (Psalm 119:105)

The more you know of God's Word, the more effectively
you can pray with confidence.

April 20

God's Love

Humble yourselves, therefore, under God's mighty hand that he may lift you up in due time. Cast all your anxiety on him because he cares for you.

I Peter 5:6-7

We often worry about our position or status, hoping to be recognized for who we are or for what we do. Peter reminds us to focus on God's recognition, that He may lift us up. He is the one who cares for us. It takes humility to understand how much He cares. As we realize how dependent we are on God, day by day, and admit our need, He will bear our burdens and struggles. He will give us strength and direction.

Casting our cares on Him is not a passive, taking for granted thought, but an action on our part of "letting go and letting God" do His work. A progressive growth in Him.

Don't submit to circumstances but God who controls circumstances.

April 21

The Word

You must teach what is in accord with sound doctrine.
Titus 2:1 NIV

Believers must be grounded in the truth of God's Word so they will not be deceived by false teachers. We need to study the Bible, learn theology, apply biblical principles and do what we learn. We need wisdom and discernment to control our will, our tongue and our desires, so we can be examples of godliness.

> "You can tell but never teach
> Unless you practice what you preach."

The one who teaches has a great responsibility to practice integrity—soundness of speech—which comes from careful Bible study and being sensitive to the Holy Spirit.

Christ's death redeemed me from the captivity of sin and death. His resurrection power, at work in me, purifies me from sin's influence as I grow in Christ.

April 22

Hope

Praise be to the God and Father of our Lord Jesus Christ! In his great mercy he has given us new birth into a living hope through the resurrection of Jesus Christ from the dead.

I Peter 1:3

New birth refers to our spiritual birth—regeneration, regened—through the Holy Spirit placing us into the family of God. This is a living hope of eternal life, not just for the future but for now as Christ lives in us daily, to enable us to endure whatever we must face on this earth.

Trials teach us patience as we grow in our faith, trusting the indwelling power of God's Holy Spirit to help us through every situation. God's grace is sufficient for each need.

What the unbeliever gets may last a lifetime if he is lucky. What we get from following God will last forever.

April 23

God's Gift

*For the wages of sin is death, but the gift of God is
eternal life in Christ Jesus our Lord.*
Romans 6:23

When we think of wages we relate it to what we have
earned—we deserve it. On the other hand we consider
a gift as something not earned—undeserved.

We would never respond to someone who presented us
with a gift, by saying, "I can't accept your gift unless I
pay you for it."

Eternal life in Christ Jesus is offered to us as a gift from
God, and yet many refuse to accept His gift. He desires
we accept it graciously with joy and thanksgiving. They
not only reject the gift but also the Giver.

Others accept the gift but continue trying to repay the
Giver, not realizing their efforts are in vain.

Our salvation is a gift from God because of His grace
and mercy, not because of anything we have done or
can do. All He wants is our love and devotion to Him
expressed through our obedience.

April 24

God's Promises

*His divine power has given us everything we need for
life and godliness through our knowledge of Him who
called us by his own glory and goodness. Through these
he has given us his very great and precious promises,
so that through them you may participate in the divine
nature and escape the corruption in the world caused by
evil desires.*

II Peter 1:3-4 NIV

Though the power of the indwelling Holy Spirit we are able to be all and do all that God expects of us. All that He calls us to be and do, He does in and through us. He has given us great and precious promises to claim as we participate in His divine nature through His Holy Spirit. His power enables us to overcome the world, the flesh and the devil.

We have the responsibility to appropriate this power daily as we obey God's Word and principles.

Our Lord only promises us strength to do His will. If we drive ourselves beyond that point we're on our own. Much of our emotional turmoil, spiritual dullness and physical illness can be traced to bodies that are too tired.

April 25

Humility

Do nothing out of selfish ambition or vain conceit, but in humility consider others better than yourselves. Each of you should look not only to your own interest, but also to the interest of others.

Philippians 2:3-4 NIV

Being humble involves having a true perspective of ourselves. (Romans 12:3—Do not think of yourselves more highly than you ought). It does not mean that we should put ourselves down. By God's grace we have been saved and therefore we have worth in God's kingdom.

We are not to dwell on man's approval but on God's approval, seeking to be what He wants us to be, where He wants us to be, when He wants us to be.

> Then we are guided by the Holy Spirit:
> The words of Christ will be in my mind,
> The love of Christ will be behind my actions,
> The power of Christ will help control my desires.

True humility cannot happen until we become self-forgetful. When you have to think about being humble you're not there yet.

April 26

Goodness

*So in everything, do to others what you would have them
do to you, for this sums up the Law and the Prophets.*
Matthew 7:12 NIV

This is what we refer to as the Golden Rule. Some
religions state it negatively: "Don't do to others what
you don't want done to you." We may think it means
the same, however we say it, but Jesus made it more
significant by stating it positively. It may be easier
for us to refrain from harming others than to take the
initiative in doing something good for them. Jesus saw
the Golden Rule as an active expression of goodness
and mercy.

Jesus said that He didn't come to do away with the
Law but to give it a "fuller meaning."

Casual friends are there when they need you.
Closest friends are there when you need them.

April 27

Love

The entire law is summed up in a single command:
Love your neighbor as yourself.
Galatians 5:14

Love—what is love? Love cannot be defined—it can only be experienced and expressed. The only definition: God is Love. His nature is love. His Word is love. His actions are an expression of His love. The Bible is a book about love—God's love for His creation—man's love for God and love for one another.

We often overlook the words "as yourself," in this verse, but we cannot love the Lord or anyone else unless we love our own being. We are to respect ourselves as a child of God, created for fellowship with Him. Our self-worth is rooted in the fact that we have a relationship with God. He has a plan for us and He has given us His Holy Spirit to enable us to fulfill that plan.

If we dislike ourselves, we may feel unworthy of God and fail to approach Him as Father. When we have a true concept of who we are in Christ, then we can exercise our God-given abilities to reach our full potential for Him.

As we recognize our worth and learn to love the person God created us to be, we can then love others as God has created them.

April 28

Faith

*Therefore, since we have been justified through faith,
we have peace with God through our Lord Jesus Christ,
through whom we have gained access by faith into this
grace in which we now stand. And we rejoice in the
hope of the glory of God.*
Romans 5:1-2

Faith, hope and love are at the heart of the Christian life. Our relationship with God begins with faith which brought us peace with God through the death and resurrection of our Lord Jesus Christ. This takes care of our past. This took place because of God's love for us.

Through faith we now stand in God's grace which enables us to overcome in the present. God's love fills our lives and gives us the ability to reach out to others.

We can rejoice in our hope of what God has for our future—the hope of God's glory—our glorification in eternity with Him.

> Christ in me, the hope of glory,
> No fear within my soul.
> I trust in God's unfailing love,
> And faithful promises of old.

April 29

Servanthood

Your attitude should be the same as that of Jesus Christ,
who, being in very nature God, did not consider equality
with God something to be grasped, but made himself
nothing, taking the very nature of a servant, being made
in human likeness.
Philippians 2:5-7

Our human attitude is that we have certain rights and
we want those rights respected. Jesus had a different
attitude. Even though He was God, Creator of all, He
was willing to let go of His rights and become a servant,
totally dependent upon the Father and His will.

As sovereign He chose to lay aside the right to His
glory and power in order to identify with humanity.
He became subject to place, time and other limitations
of mankind. He willingly depended upon the Holy
Spirit to work through Him as the Father's Servant.
He did nothing except in obedience to the Father's will.
What made His humanity unique was His sinlessness,
though He was "tempted in every way just as we are."
(Hebrews 4:15)

We, as believers, are indwelt by the Holy Spirit to
enable us to overcome temptation, as Jesus did. We
have His Name, His Word and His blood to protect us.

The willingness of Jesus to serve the Father is our
example to serve others in obedience to Him.

April 30

Worship

*God is Spirit, and his worshipers must worship in spirit
and in truth.*
John 4:24 NIV

God is not a physical being limited to one place. He is
present everywhere and He can be worshiped anywhere
at any time. It's not where we worship that counts but
how we worship—our attitude.

Worship is "my spirit in communication with God,
through His spirit that dwells in me, according to His
truth—all that I am delighting in all that He is."

His Holy Spirit prays for and through me (Romans
8:26), He teaches me the Word (John 13:26), and He
makes God's love real in my life (Romans 5:5).

"My spirituality cannot be measured by my outside
actions, seen by others, but by my inside attitudes seen
by God." If my inside is pure then the outside will be
pleasing to God and others.

It is good to be strong in body and strong in mind, but
far more important to be strong in the Spirit.

May

May 1

God's Will

In his heart man plans his course but the Lord
determines his steps.
Proverbs 16:9 NIV

Our human nature desires to be in control of our personal life. This was first demonstrated in the life of Adam and Eve and continues today. We refer to it as being "independent." We need to realize that there is no such state of man for we are totally dependent upon God. God has also ordained that we are dependent upon one another.

We make our plans and ask God to bless them, then we go on our merry way and forget God. God desires that we seek Him first and get His direction. His plans are always for our good.

It's amazing how much we trust technology today but doubt God's ability to guide us. If cars can be directed by satellite, in space, why should we question God's direction in our lives? Could the problem be that we don't want to let go of the steering wheel?

May 2

God's Will

*And we know that god causes all things to work together
for good to those who love God, to those who are called
according to his purpose.*
Romans 8:25 NAS

Because of different translations of the Bible, we
sometimes misquote or misinterpret the Scriptures.
For this reason we need to study all of God's Word and
allow the Holy Spirit to guide us in an understanding
of it.

As we consider this verse that Paul has written, it
doesn't say that God causes all things, for God does not
cause evil—He allows it—but He often causes evil to
work for good in spite of circumstances. He causes all
things—good and bad—to work together in bringing
fulfillment to His plan and purpose for us, His children.
That plan includes our being conformed to the image of
(becoming like) Christ, for His glory.

God's order is not to change conditions in order to
change people but to change people in order to change
conditions.

May 3

God's Love

*May the grace of the Lord Jesus Christ, and the love of
God, and the fellowship of the Holy Spirit be with you
all.*

II Corinthians 13:14 NIV

Paul had been communicating with the Church at
Corinth about the sin within the Church, moral and
spiritual conditions. This was to be his final blessing
and it included the Trinity—the Father, the Son and
the Holy Spirit.

He could have refused any contact until they dealt with
the situation but he loved them and kept reaching out
with the love of Christ.

Sometimes we refer to "tough love," when we must
confront those we care about, especially when they are
ruining their lives with sin. But we must approach
them in a spirit of love, concern and forgiveness.

A wrong approach –legalistic attitude, or turn away
from them—can destroy a loving, trusting relationship.

Dealing with these situations can drain us emotionally
but it's the only Christlike way to deal with others.

May 4

Peace

*You will keep in perfect peace him whose mind is
steadfast, because he trusts in you.*
Isaiah 26:3 NIV

The world is in turmoil all around us and we are
searching for answers to all of life's problems. We will
always have problems but God tells us how to have
peace in the midst of problems. Keep our focus on Him
who is the answer. Some things to consider that can
keep us steadfast:

1) Accept who and where we are as God created
us. He chose the time and place we would be
born, determined what we would look like and
gave us our individuality, talents and spiritual
gifts.

2) Realize that God has a purpose and plan for our
life. (Proverbs 3:5-6)

3) Know that we belong to Him. He has accepted
us as His child in the Lord Jesus Christ.
Nothing can change that. (John 10)

4) Keep a clear conscience. Confess and repent of
sins. (I John 1:9)

5) Rejoice and rest in Him.

May 5

My Purpose

As you sent me into the world, I have sent them into the world.
John 17:18 NIV

As the Father sent me, I am sending you.
John 20:21 NIV

Christ came into the world to reveal the Father to the world. Jesus told Philip, "He that has seen me has seen the Father." "I and the Father are one." (John 10:30) This is a clear statement of Jesus' divinity. Jesus and the Father are not the same person but they are one in essence and nature. Jesus said that He always did what pleased the Father.

Christ told His disciples that He was sending them in the same way, to make Himself known to the world, as the Son of God, Savior of the world. This would be accomplished as the Holy Spirit works in and through the life of the believer to transform his character and nature to be conformed to the character and nature of Christ.

Our responsibility is to allow the Holy Spirit the freedom to work in our life according to the will of the Father.

May 6

God's Possession

For ye are bought with a price: therefore, glorify God in your body, and in your spirit, which are God's.

I Corinthians 6:20 KJV

We often hear someone say, "It's my body, I'll do what I please with it." God created us to glorify Himself, (to be an expression of His character and nature) and He loves us unconditionally, but He has given us the freedom to make choices. God, however, determines the consequences of those choices.

When man chose to separate himself from God, through disobedience, God chose to buy him back. He gave His Son, the Lord Jesus Christ, to pay the penalty (the consequences) of man's sin, which was death, and through Christ He gave man life eternal.

God not only created us but He has recreated us so we belong to Him (twice-born).

When we buy something we like to think that it is worth what we pay for it. We like a good return on our investment.

God desires a good return on His investment in us—that our lives reflect His likeness. His Holy Spirit indwells us to enable us to do that. We should respect our body as the Temple of the Holy Spirit.

I should ask myself daily, "Am I just spending life or am I investing it for the Lord?"

May 7

The Word

*Blessed is the man who does not walk in the counsel
of the wicked or stand in the way of sinners or sit in
the seat of mockers. But his delight is in the law of the
Lord, and on his law he meditates day and night.*

Psalm 1:1-2 NIV

This is God's instruction for happiness, which depends on happenings (circumstances). We can control many of our circumstances by the choices we make. We can always choose our response to circumstances.

We can learn God's ways and how to follow Him by meditating on His Word. Meditating means spending time reading and thinking about what we have read. Then asking how we should change so we're living as God wants. If we would follow God more closely, we must know what He says.

The more we know of God's Word, the more resources we will have to guide us in our daily decisions.

May 8

God's Sovereignty

*The Lord gave and the Lord has taken away; may the
name of the Lord be praised.*
Job 1:21b NIV

We are prone to think that God's blessings involve
everything that we desire; what we think is good and
will make us happy. So we pray that God will bless us
and that He will bless our loved ones and friends. We
fail to consider that what may be our idea of a blessing
may not be God's idea. He knows what is best for us
and what is necessary to work that in our lives.

"We cannot know the sweetness of Christ until we
experience the bitterness of trials."

Job had learned this truth.

God may have to remove something from our life before
He can bless us with His best. In some situations His
best requires taking something away.

We develop attitudes, habits, relationships that hinder
our walk with the Lord and He has to remove these to
get our attention. Only when "self" becomes helpless,
are we willing to turn to Him for help and he is able to
"bless" us.

May 9

Patience

*And so after waiting patiently, Abraham received what
was promised.*
Hebrews 6:15 NIV

We often hear the statement, "Lord, give me patience
and I need it now." We don't have time for patience
in this world of "instant" everything. Patience is not
a natural inclination—it is a God-given disposition
that comes through practice. It is a hard lesson to
learn because it often involves trials and temptations.
(Hebrews 10:36)

Abraham waited twenty-five years for a son. He tried
to help God by taking a shortcut but it caused much
heartache and trouble. God's timing is always perfect.

> I will trust while I wait
> For my God is never late.

When you become impatient in a situation or feel
pressured to make a hasty decision, you may want
to consider—the Holy Spirit is always gentle in His
moving. God tells us over and over to "wait on Him."
Only Satan is happy when we make a mistake.

Part of the blessing is the trust and wisdom gained
while waiting.

May 10

Fear

Do not fear for I am with you; do not anxiously look about you, for I am your God. I will strengthen you, surely I will help you. Surely I will uphold you with my righteous right hand.

Isaiah 41:10 NAS

We cannot control circumstances, which often cause fear, but we can choose how we respond to circumstances.

We can dwell on negative thoughts, of possibilities, and try to reason what we should do or we can respond according to Philippians 4:6-7. "Do not be anxious about anything, but in everything, by prayer and petition, with thanksgiving; present your request to God. And the peace of God, which transcends all understanding will guard your hearts and minds in Christ Jesus."

Fear does not come from God and as believers He has given us authority and power, in Jesus name, to reject what isn't from Him.

Satan uses fear as one of His tools to discourage and defeat Christians. Resist Him in the name of Jesus!

May 11

Stay Alert

*So, if you think you are standing firm, be careful that
you don't fall!*
I Corinthians 10:12 NIV

In our world of pressures today we easily ignore or
forget the lessons of the past. It has been said that
"experience is what we get when we don't get what
we want." Too many times we don't learn from our
experiences so we continue a lifestyle of defeat.

We face a challenging situation and ask God for help in
knowing what to do. He gives us wisdom and direction
in our decisions and everything works out for our good.
We rejoice and praise God for His goodness.

These are the times when we can become vulnerable
to Satan's subtle attacks—maybe an insignificant
temptation, and we push it aside as not important.
We don't really need to bother God about it for we can
handle it.

Life moves along as usual and suddenly things fall
apart and we can't understand why.

Past victories do not guarantee future successes. Every
day is a new opportunity to seek God's will and wisdom
in our life, no matter how small the decisions are.

Our communion with Him is priceless!

May 12

Our Legacy

Only be careful, and watch yourselves closely so that you do not forget the things your eyes have seen or let them slip from your heart as long as you live. Teach them to your children and to their children after them.
Deuteronomy 4:9 NIV

The most valuable "possession" believers can leave to family and friends is faith in Jesus Christ. They must choose to trust in the Lord themselves but they are encouraged as they see and hear how He works in our life.

Children must be taught that the most important thing in their life is their relationship with God and how to have that relationship and nurture it day by day.

God has a purpose and plan for each of us and He will provide all that is needed to fulfill that plan. Our "testimony" is our "legacy" that we leave for our family and friends.

May 13

Our Example

*These commands that I give you today are to be upon
your hearts. Impress them upon your children. Talk
about them when you sit at home and when you walk
along the road, when you lie down and when you get up.*
Deuteronomy 6:6-7 NIV

God's word emphasizes the importance of parents
teaching the Bible to their children. Too often we have
left that responsibility to the church. Eternal truths
are best taught and learned in a God-fearing home
by loving parents. Religious education should be life-
oriented, not information-oriented.

If we want our children to follow God we must make
God a part of our daily life, teaching them to see God in
all aspects of life, not just what is church-related.

> We can tell but never teach
> Unless we practice what we preach.

We cannot share what we do not have. If our relationship
with Christ is not real and exciting we cannot teach
our children about intimacy with God.

"Example is more caught than taught."

May 14

Parents Responsibility

Train a child in the way he should go, and when he is old he will not turn from it.
Proverbs 22:6 NIV

Fathers, do not exasperate your children; instead, bring them up in the training and instruction of the Lord.
Ephesians 6:4 NIV

What does it mean to train a child in the way he should go? Teaching involves information while training comes through experience. Both are necessary to fulfill our responsibility as parents. Both involve discipline.

Parenting is not easy. It takes patience, love and understanding along with godly wisdom. Children and parents have a responsibility to one another, considering the other's interest and an attitude of submission. Children are to honor their parents and parents are to gently care for their children.

Each person is unique from birth and God has His plan for each child. When we try to fit everybody into our mold, we can cause frustration and anger in relationships. The instruction of the Lord, through His Word, must be our guideline - our map - pointing us in the way we should go as we direct our children.

May 15

Seeking God

*Show me your ways, O Lord, teach me your paths; guide
me in your truth and teach me, for you are God my
Savior, and my hope is in you all day long.*
Psalm 25:4-5 NIV

How great is your desire to know God's Word, His will,
His ways? This desire must come from a heart-seeking
God, being mindful of our dependence on Him.

God's primary guidance comes from His Word,
the Bible. As we read and learn His Word we gain
knowledge and wisdom in God's direction for our lives.
When we obey Him He gives us the ability to know His
ways—to see from his perspective—and as we wait on
Him we experience the peace of knowing that He is in
control.

When others observe what God is doing in our lives
they will see that Christ is real and He will be glorified.

May 16

God

You shall have no other gods before me.
Deuteronomy 5:7

This is God Almighty, God of all creation speaking. He deserves our complete allegiance for we are totally dependent on Him. He is the source of our being—our life. Apart from Him we are nothing.

When we think of other gods we usually associate them with paganism. We fail to realize how subtle the temptation is to build our lives around something other than the one true God. As a result we can find ourselves worshiping other gods—power, popularity, money, pleasure or even family. Anything we put before God can become a god. Whatever or whoever comes first in our life is our god.

Our love for God should be the motive for everything we do.

May 17

The Christian Life

And now these three remain: faith, hope and love. But the greatest of these is love.

I Corinthians 13:13

Faith, hope and love are at the heart of the Christian life. Our relationship with God begins with faith, which helps us realize that we are delivered from our past by Christ's death. (Romans 4:25)

"Therefore, since we have been justified through faith, we have peace with God through our Lord Jesus Christ, through whom we have gained access by faith into this grace in which we now stand. And we rejoice in the hope of the glory of God." (Romans 5:1-2)

Hope grows as we learn all that God has in mind for us; it gives us the promise of the future. And god's love fills our lives and gives us the ability to reach out to others.

Faith is the foundation and content of God's message; hope is the attitude and focus; love is the action. When faith and hope are in line you're free to love completely because you understand how God loves. (Ephesians 2:17-18)

By faith, we stand in God's grace because of the love of Christ. We enjoy peace and rejoice in the hope of the glory of God.

May 18

My Prayer
(Taken from Psalm 71)

You have been my hope, O Sovereign Lord, my confidence since my youth. From birth I have relied on you; you brought me forth from my mother's womb. I will ever praise you. You will not cast me away when I am old, nor forsake me when my strength is gone. I will always have hope; I will praise you more and more. Since my youth, O God, you have taught me and to this day I declare your marvelous works. Even when I am old and gray you will not forsake, O God, till I declare your power to the next generation, your might to all who come. Though you have made me see troubles, many and bitter, you always restore my life again—from the depths of the earth you will again bring me up. My lips will shout for joy when I sing praise to you—I whom you have redeemed. I will praise you for your faithfulness, O my God!

May 19

Waiting on God

*Show me our way, O Lord, teach me your paths; guide
me in your truth and teach me, for you are God my
Savior, and my hope is in you all day long.*
Psalm 25:4 NIV

I must want to be guided and I must realize that God's primary guidance system is His Word. Psalm 119 tells of the endless knowledge found in God's Word. By reading it and learning from it, I will gain wisdom to perceive God's direction for my life. I cannot demand answers from God but I can ask for directions. When I am willing to seek God, learn from His Word and obey His commands, then I can expect His guidance.

There can be obstacles that hinder the answer:

Temptation to follow my own schedule. Impatience may cause me to run ahead of God or insecurity may lead me to lag behind.

Pressure from others may influence me or fear of failure. My focus must be on pleasing God, not people.

A lifestyle that seeks quietness before God will develop intimacy with Him and encourage my faith in Him.

May 20

Resurrection

*If only for this life we have hope in Christ, we are to be
pitied more than all men.*
I Corinthians 15:19 NIV

A person's attitude concerning the resurrection is
important because it not only impacts our faith but our
witness also. There would be no point in telling others
about Jesus if He remained in the grave.

Without Christ's resurrection, we have no hope of
eternity, no saving Lord, no powerful word and a dead
faith. The only basis for eternal hope is receiving
Christ's sacrificial death for sin and believing He
conquered sin and death and rose victorious over the
grave and Satan.

Christ died to save me—He lives to keep me. My
security is in Him!

May 21

God's Love

A new commandment I give you: Love one another.
As I have loved you, so you must love one another. By
this all men will know that you are my disciples, if you
love one another.
John 13:34-35 NIV

Jesus was on His way to the cross to die, as the perfect sacrifice, for the sin of all mankind. He knew all that was going to happen—that Judas would betray Him and Peter would deny Him, but He loved them regardless of what they would do. He knows what we will do to hurt Him and yet He loves us unconditionally and He always forgives when we ask Him.

We are to be living examples of Jesus' love for us. Love is more than simply warm feelings; it's an attitude that reveals itself in actions. How?

By helping when it is not convenient.
By giving when it hurts.
By accepting hurt from others without fighting back.
By a spirit of acceptance and forgiveness.

This is not a natural love but a supernatural "fruit of the Spirit." (Galatians 5:23) Our pattern is I Corinthians 13.

May 22

Setting Goals

*The eye is the lamp of the body. If your eyes are good,
your whole body will be full of light. But if your eyes are
bad, your whole body will be full of darkness. If then the
light within you is darkness, how great is that darkness.*
Matthew 6:22-23 NIV

Spiritual vision is our capacity to see clearly what God
wants us to do and to see the world from His point
of view. This spiritual insight can be easily clouded.
Self-serving desires, interest and goals can block that
vision. Serving God is the best way to restore it. A
"good" eye is one that is fixed on God.

As we spend time in prayer and Bible study, the Holy
Spirit weaves Himself in and through our conscience.
It becomes a type of filter through which I process my
behavior and decisions.

If I do something that causes "static" in my conscience,
that is God's way of telling me to "stop and consider."
The choice may be mine—not God's. My conscience
is a God-given "warning system." I need to heed the
"alert" it sends.

May 23

God's Presence

*The Lord is my light and my salvation—whom shall I
fear? The Lord is the stronghold of my life—of whom
shall I be afraid?*

Psalm 27:1 NIV

The lord is my light, therefore He guides me in every situation.

The Lord is my salvation, therefore He protects me from the evil one.

The Lord is my stronghold, therefore He is my refuge and strength.

David's prayer was to dwell in the house of the Lord all of his life and to gaze upon His beauty. There was peace in the presence of God for David. (v. 4)

Christ is our Peace. (Ephesians 2:14) He has defeated our true enemies—Satan and death. He set us free from the slavery of sin; the Devil lost control of our lives. We no longer face eternal separation from God but we will enjoy His presence forever.

Nothing can separate us from Him. (Romans 8:38-39) We can live free from fear!

May 24

Fear

For God did not give us a spirit of timidity, but a spirit of power, of love and of self-discipline.
II Timothy 1:7 NIV

Timothy was a young pastor. He was facing opposition to his ministry because of his age, his message and his association with Paul. Paul sought to encourage him in his faith by reminding him of who he was in Christ.

He had the power of the Holy Spirit indwelling him, the love of Christ motivating him and the faith to discipline himself in his ministry.

There are two kinds of fear: healthy and unhealthy.

(1)   Healthy fear involves a preventive, protective anxiety of danger that warns us of harm. It also involves a proper fear (reverence) of God which leads to a sense of awe because of who He is, and a desire to honor Him.

(2)   Unhealthy fear causes us to feel uneasy, threatened. Much of this type of fear has to do with imagination. We get caught up in "what if" thinking. This kind of fear can hinder God's desire for His best in our life. This type of fear is not from God but from Satan whose goal is to defeat us.

"Faith conquers fear."

May 25

Humility

Humble yourselves before the Lord, and he will lift you up.
James 45:10 NIV; I Peter 5:6 NIV

Most of us have a problem when it comes to humility. God knows this and He reminds us, in His Word, what He thinks of pride. (James 4:6)

Our worth comes from God alone for "in Him we live and move and have our being." Apart from Him we are nothing and can do nothing. He is our life and breath.

To be humble involves working in His power according to His direction, not my own efforts or ideas.

The human goal is to be independent in this world—not "beholden" to anyone. We forget that God created man for fellowship with Him and with one another. Submit and love are attitudes we are to express in our relationships.

When we acknowledge our dependence upon God and others, then we can learn to walk in humility, graciously accepting their love and concern.

May 26

Contentment

Keep your lives free from the love of money and be content with what you have, because God has said, Never will I leave you, never will I forsake you.

Hebrews 13:5 NIV

Contentment is a word seldom used today and less practiced. Our mindset is focused on change and how we can bring it about. Someone has said, "If you're not content with what you have, you will not be content with what you get." There is great truth in this statement, because when we think of "how much is enough," our thought is "just a little bit more."

One of the greatest causes of discontentment is the "love of money," which is a "root" of all kinds of evil. (I Timothy 6:10)

To get rid of a weed you destroy the root. To get rid of greed you control the desire. When we become materialistic we are saying by our actions, that God can't or won't take care of our needs.

God has promised never to forsake us and when we realize His sufficiency for our needs we can learn to trust Him and be content with the way He provides.

May 27

God Remembers

*Then those who feared the Lord talked with each
other, and the Lord listened and heard. A scroll of
remembrance was written in his presence concerning
those who feared the Lord and honored his name.*

Malachi 3:16

In verse 6 God reminded His people, "I the Lord never
change."

People change—sometime for better and sometime
for worse. We choose according to our desires and we
experience the consequences of our choices.

God never changes and God never forgets. He may
choose not to remember, as He has concerning our sin
(Jeremiah 31:34), but there is a difference in forgetting
and choosing not to remember.

The Lord knows those who are His, who fear and honor
Him. His desire is that all turn to Him and honor His
name.

May 28

Prayer

*The end of all things is near. Therefore be clear-minded
and self-controlled so that you can pray.*
I Peter 4:7 NIV

We don't know when Christ will be coming but we
know He is coming again because of His Word and He
is faithful to His promises. Getting ready to meet Him
involves growing in love for God and others. One of
the ways we do this is through prayer and reaching
out to others. We will spend eternity with other people.
We need to invest our time and talents where they will
make an eternal difference.

Peter is saying there are some conditions necessary if
we are to pray effectively. Clear-minded means to have
no unconfessed sin, no clutter of misplaced priorities,
but a conscience clear and transparent before God.

Self-controlled means choosing to allow the Holy Spirit
to be in control, denying selfish attitudes and actions.

When we prepare ourselves mentally and spiritually
we can come before the throne of grace boldly, guided
by the Holy Spirit, knowing God will hear and answer.

May 29

God's Love

In him we have redemption through his blood, the
forgiveness of sins in accordance with the riches of
God's grace that he lavished on us with all wisdom and
understanding.
Ephesians 1:7 NIV

This verse is loaded with God's expression of love and goodness poured out upon us. In verse 3, Paul says God has blessed us in the heavenly realms with every spiritual blessing in Christ.

In Christ we have all the benefits of knowing God— salvation, adoption, forgiveness, insight, gifts of the Spirit, power, hope of eternity with Christ. Because of our intimate relationship with Christ we can enjoy these blessings now.

The "heavenly realms" means these blessings are eternal, not temporal. We did not influence God's decision to save us. It was His plan, in His mind, long before we existed.

Two great truths are based on the death of Christ— redemption and forgiveness of sins—because of God's grace flooding our soul.

May 30

Discipline

Our fathers disciplined us for a little while as they thought best; but God disciplines us for our good, that we may share in His holiness.
Hebrews 12:10-11

It is never pleasant to be corrected or disciplined by God, but His discipline is a sign of His great love for us. Our response should be, "Lord, what are you trying to teach me?"

One of His purposes is to develop personal righteousness in us. He prunes away the "dead wood"—attitudes, behaviors, and relationships that do not fit a child of God. (Ephesians 4:25, 29, 31)

As we depend on Him in times of suffering, He can manifest His life in us as an example for others. As Christ's followers, we are to be living examples of His character. This may mean forgiving our enemies, bearing our burdens with patience as finding joy in the midst of sorrow.

Our suffering is being used for God's eternal purposes.

May 31

Lord of All

He is the image of the invisible God, the firstborn over all creation. All things were created by Him and for Him.
Colossians 1:15-16

This is one of the strongest statements, found in the Bible, about the divine nature of Christ. Jesus is not only equal to God, He is God. He not only reflects God but He reveals God to us. As the firstborn over all creation, He has all power and authority. He is Lord of all.

As believers we must believe in the deity of Christ (that He is God), or our Christian faith is hollow, misdirected and meaningless. This is a central truth of Christianity.

The only way I can know God in His fullness is to know Jesus Christ as He is—to behold His glory and be transformed into His likeness.

June

June 1

God is Faithful

*As the Scripture says, anyone who trusts in Him will
never be put to shame.*
Romans 10:11

God is faithful. He will do what He says He will do—
those who call on Him will be saved. He will never fail
those who trust and believe in Him.

Psalm 25:3 says, "No one whose hope is in you will
ever be put to shame." God's best for us is His heart's
desire, and as He works that in our life, He is glorified.

Our responsibility is to be sensitive to His leading and
to be obedient and trust His will, His way and His
Word. His timing is always perfect. We need wisdom
and patience to wait on Him.

Fully trusting in God's love for us, we will experience
His best as He glorifies Himself through us.

> Show me your ways, O Lord,
> Teach me your paths;
> Guide me in your truth and teach me,
> For you are God my Savior, and my
> Hope is in you all day long.
> Psalm 25:4-5

June 2

God is Sovereign

The Lord foils the plans of the nations; he thwarts the purposes of the peoples. But the plans of the Lord stand firm forever, the purposes of his heart through all generations.
Psalm 33:10-11

God is sovereign and He is faithful. There is much concern and indecision in our nation today as we face the coming election of a president. We are told in I Timothy 2:1, to pray for our nation and leaders. This is our responsibility as we seek God's wisdom in making decisions. We are to be obedient to His leading and leave the results to Him.

"The king's heart is in the hands of the Lord; he directs it like a water course wherever he pleases." (Proverbs 21:1)

There are two elements in man's relationship to God;

God's revelation and man's response.

Faith: the soul daring to go where the mind cannot think.

June 3

God's Goodness

Why are you downcast, O my soul? Why so disturbed within me? Put your hope in God, for I will yet praise him, my Savior and my God.

Psalm 42:5a

Depression is one of the most common emotional ailments. Discouragement is a choice and in this state of mind we can allow our circumstances to consume us.

We may have physical, financial or family problems but we can choose how we will respond to our situation. One antidote for depression is to focus on God's goodness. This will take your mind off your problem and give you hope that it will improve as you cast your cares on Him. (I Peter 5:7)

When you feel lonely or depressed, meditate on God's kindness and love. Spend time in God's Word seeking direction and pray for God's joy to be your strength to overcome.

June 4

Holiness

You have been set free from sin and have become salves of righteousness   Romans 6:18

But now that you have been set free from sin and have become salves to God, the benefit you reap leads to holiness, and the result is eternal life.
Romans 6:22

But now that you have been set free from sin and have become salves to God, the benefit you reap leads to holiness, and the result is eternal life.
Romans 6:22

Christ died to pay the penalty for sin. When I accepted Christ as my Savior He freed me from the penalty of sin and gave me the choice to become His slave. As I obey Him, as my Master, He gives me power to overcome sin and live a life of righteousness which leads to holiness. The result will be freedom from the presence of sin in eternity.

Life on this earth is made up of choices. We are free to choose between two masters but we are not free to control the consequences of our choice.

Each master pays with his own currency.

Satan—the currency of sin, which is death.
Christ—the currency of righteousness , which is life.

June 5

God's Grace

*I do not set aside the grace of God, for if righteousness
could be gained through the law, Christ died for
nothing.*
Galatians 2:21 NIV

One of the greatest hindrances to the personal
acceptance of Jesus Christ is pride. We are a society
who delights in boasting—what we know, who we
know, where we go and what we have.

Paul said, "May I never boast except in the cross of our
Lord Jesus Christ, through which the world has been
crucified to me, and I to the world." (Galatians 6:4)

We have a problem acknowledging our dependence
upon Jesus alone for our salvation, and that His death
was sufficient to pay the penalty for our sin, as a gift of
eternal life.

If we could be saved by being good, then Christ did not
have to die.

Only "The Way of The Cross Leads Home!"

"Let him who boast, boast in the Lord." (I Corinthians
1:31)

June 6

Twice-Born

Jesus declared, "I tell you the truth, no one can see the kingdom of God unless he is born again."

Flesh gives birth to flesh, but the spirit gives birth to spirit.
John 3:3, 6 NIV

What does it mean to be born again?

Regeneration is the transformation of an individual, by the Holy Spirit, into a new creation. (II Corinthians 5:17) We become a new creature. We receive our physical genes from our biological parents, at physical birth. Through regeneration we received our spiritual genes (regened) from our Spiritual Father, at spiritual birth.

We are born again, from above, into the Family of God. His Holy Spirit indwells our spirit, to enable us to be conformed to the likeness of Christ, as members of His Kingdom. (New DNA) (II Corinthians 3:18)

June 7

Testing

See, I have refined you, though not as silver; I have tested you in the furnace of affliction.
Isaiah 48:10 NIV

Why does a loving Father allow His children to go through suffering, pain and unpleasant experiences? God meets us where we are but He loves us too much to leave us there. He helps us to grow more and more like His Son. (II Corinthians 3:18)

Rather than complain we should turn to God in faith for strength to endure. (Romans 5:3) For without the testing we would never know how God can work through our trials to help us grow in our faith in Him.

Paul tells us that in the future we will "become," but until then we are to "overcome," Our problems will develop perseverance—which in turn will strengthen character, deepen our trust in God and increase our confidence for the future.

June 8

God's Providence

*And we know that in all things God works for the good
of those who love Him, who have been called according
to His purpose.*
Romans 8:28

God works in "all things" for our good. It doesn't mean that bad things will not come our way but God is sovereign and He can work through bad experiences to bring good into our live.

God is not working in our life to make us happy but to make us holy, to fulfill his purpose. He works good in the lives of those who love Him. Those who are "called" are those the Holy Spirit convinces and enables to receive Christ.

These individuals have a new perspective, a new mind-set on life. They trust in God, not treasures; they look for their security in heaven, not on earth; they learn to accept, not resent pain and persecution, because God is with them.

June 9

Hope

*Praise be to the God and Father of our Lord Jesus
Christ! In his great mercy he has given us new birth into
a living hope through the resurrection of Jesus Christ
from the dead.*

I Peter 1:3

Our hope is a living hope, in a living person, Jesus Christ. Our hope is not only for the future but "eternal life" began when we trusted Christ as our Savior, and became a member of God's family.

Our hope is an eternal hope and we know that whatever we face here on earth, pain or trials, is only temporary and eventually we'll live with Christ in eternity. God will help us remain true to our faith in Him through whatever difficult times we experience.

Trials teach us patience (Romans 5:3-4; James 1:2-3), and helps us to become the persons God called us to be.

June 10

Holiness

Therefore, prepare your minds for action; be self-controlled; set your hope fully on the grace to be given you when Jesus Christ is revealed—for it is written: Be holy, because I am holy.

When we think of the return of Christ, it should motivate us to live for Him. Our desires should be different to those of the world around us, physically, mentally and spiritually. As believers we have been transformed (set apart), to be holy not only in position but also in practice.

Peter tells us the way to do that is, first, prepare your mind (mentally alert), discipline yourself (self-control), focus on Christ (our hope).

Holiness means being totally devoted or dedicated to God—set apart for His special use and against sin and its influence. The Holy Spirit will enable us to practice holiness when we set our mind on Him.

June 11

Comfort

Praise be to the God and Father of our Lord Jesus Christ, the Father of compassion and the God of all comfort, who comforts us in all our troubles, so that we can comfort those in any trouble with the comfort we ourselves have received from God.
II Corinthians 1:3-4 NIV

Many think that when God comforts us that our troubles should go away. Notice that we are told that God comforts us "in" our troubles—not so they would go away but so we can comfort others.

Being comforted can mean receiving strength, encouragement and hope to deal with our troubles. We often depend on our own ability when life seems easy and only turn to God when we feel unable to help ourselves.

God is our source of power and we receive His help when we stay in touch with Him.

Recognizing our dependence on Him will drive us to Him when trouble comes.

June 12

Freedom—Hope

Therefore, there is now no condemnation for those who are in Christ Jesus, because through Christ Jesus the law of the Spirit of life set me free from the law of sin and death.

Romans 8:1-2 NIV

Freedom at last! Not free to do what I want to do but free to follow Christ and do the will of the Father. No longer a salve to sin and Satan, that ends in death, but a child of righteousness through the spirit of Christ, who lives forever.

God the Father had it all planned before He created the world. God the son fulfilled the plan when He died on the cross and was resurrected to life again.

God the Holy Spirit, indwelling me, is my seal of security and my hope of eternity with Christ.

June 13

God's Silence

So the sisters sent word to Jesus, "Lord, the one you love
is sick." Yet, when he heard that Lazarus was sick, he
stayed where he was two more days.
John 11:3, 6

God's silence has a message that is as important as His
speech. Sometimes we fail to get that message because
of our impatience. We expect God to act when we speak
but we are told to wait on Him. (Psalm 27:14)

The question has often been asked, "Why did Jesus wait
two days, knowing that Lazarus was sick?" Numbers
often have a significant meaning in the interpretation
of God's Word. The number two represents witness.
This was to be a miracle of Jesus' power over death,
not just sickness.

Jesus said, "I am the Way (to God), the Truth (about
God), and the Life (of God)."

Jesus would later prove that He was victorious over
death when He came forth from the grave.

June 14

Repentance

Simon Peter said to them, I am going fishing.
John 21:3

We don't know what Peter's motive was for his choice to return to fishing. It could be a good move or not a good move, depending on his motive. If his desire was to go back where he met Jesus, to renew his commitment and fellowship, then it would be a good decision.

On the other hand if he was thinking "It's not worth it, I'm going back to what I was doing before I met Jesus," then his attitude was wrong.

If my love for God has grown cold, then I need to go back where I first met Him and repent of my sins. I may be doing the work of the Lord for the wrong reason.

"The greatest competitor of devotion to Jesus is service to Him."

Oswald Chambers

June 15

Depression

Why are you downcast, O my soul? Why so disturbed within me? Put your hope in God, for I will yet praise him, my Savior and my God. Psalm 42:5

The Psalmist expressed this thought twice in eleven verses. His emotions burst forth as he remembered God's love and goodness in the past.

Depression is one of the most common emotional ailments. Meditation on God's goodness can do wonders for the depressed soul. It will focus your thoughts on God's ability to help you rather than on your inability to help yourself.

God wants us to live in His grace, rely on His strength and place our hope in Him. In this He can glorify Himself as others see what He does in and for us.

June 16

God's Presence

But the Lord stood at my side and gave me strength, -----
------ and I was delivered from the lion's mouth.
II Timothy 4:17 NIV

Paul was in prison facing death and most of his companions had deserted him. But the Lord was faithful in the past and Paul trusted Him for the future.

God doesn't always rescue us from bad situations because He may have something better. His desire may be to strengthen us through the experience.

When trouble and pain come our way we should seek to view it from God's perspective. Which is a greater demonstration of His power—changing something around me or changing something within me?

Which answer to prayer is greater—external peace because God moved something or internal peace that nothing can take away?

"What happens in me is far greater than what happens to me."

June 17

Eternal Things

Since then you have been raised with Christ, set your heart on things above, where Christ is seated at the right hand of God. Set your minds on things above, not on earthly things.
Colossians 3:1-2

Setting our hearts—putting heaven's priorities into daily practice.

Setting our minds—concentrating on the eternal rather than the temporal.

Look at life from God's perspective and seek what He desires. We must not become too attached to what is temporary.

"Let the peace of Christ rule in your hearts." Colossians 3:15

Our hearts are the center of conflict because there are feelings and desires clash—our fears and hopes, distrust and trust, jealousy and love. To live in love leads to peace.

It is our decision as to what we set our hearts and minds on.

June 18

Our Shepherd

My sheep listen to my voice; I know them, and they
follow me.
John 10:27

Salvation involves more than going to Heaven when I die. If that were the only purpose of salvation God would take us home when we accept Christ as Savior.

As believers we must decide what we will do with Jesus after salvation. Faith in Him isn't just the way to eternal life in Heaven, it is also our way of life on this earth.

> We are to follow Him.
> We are to worship Him.
> We are to share Him.
> We are to look for his coming.

Life here is only a fleeting moment in comparison to the time we'll spend with Him in eternity.

June 19

Relationships

After David had finished talking with Saul, Jonathan became one in Spirit with David, and he loved him as himself.

I Samuel 18:1

When David and Jonathan met, they became friends at once. We were created for relationships, first with God and then with family and friends. Some relationships are more special than others.

Our spiritual relationship with the Lord must be nurtured as we stay in contact with Him through prayer and Bible study. Communion and fellowship is the secret of building a strong, healthy relationship, whether spiritual or physical.

God brings special people into our lives, with whom our spirits unite in a fruitful friendship. David and Jonathan's friendship was based on commitment to God, not just to each other. They let nothing come between them, not even career or family problems. They remained friends to the end. (I Samuel 18-20)

June 20

My Motive

Whatever you do, work at it with all your heart, as
working for the Lord, not for men.
Colossians 3:23 NIV

Much of what we do is done with a selfish attitude—
how does this affect me, is it convenient, what will
others say—rather than what the Lord would have us
do.

"In his heart a man plans his course, but the Lord
determines his steps." Proverbs 16:9 NIV

How often do we consciously consider what God has
planned for us, as we begin each day? Do we commit
our plans to Him?

We may think of some of our plans as being insignificant
but nothing we do is insignificant to the Lord, therefore
we should do it wholeheartedly.

June 21

The Holy Spirit

When the counselor comes, whom I will send to you from the Father, the Spirit of truth who goes out from the Father, he will testify about me.
John 15:26 NIV

Counselor—conveys the helping, encouraging, and strengthening work of the Holy Spirit.

Spirit of truth—points to the teaching, illuminating and reminding work of the Holy Spirit.

The Holy Spirit ministers to both the head and the heart. He is not an "it." The Holy Spirit is a "somebody."

God's Spirit possesses intelligence, will and emotions. He knows God's thoughts and illuminates the truth for us. (I Corinthians 2:10-11) He determines the spiritual gifts of believers. (I Corinthians 12:7-11)

The Holy Spirit's feelings are revealed in (Romans 15:30) which tells of His love and in (Ephesians 4:30) which warns against grieving Him.

He is a Helper and Teacher. (John 14:16, 26) He sticks closer than a brother. (Proverbs 18:24)

June 22

The Christian Life

We continually remember before our God and Father your work produced by faith, your labor prompted by love and your endurance inspired by hope in our Lord Jesus Christ.

II Thessalonians 1:3

Am I investing my life here on earth, in eternity, or just passing the time? I need to think seriously about this and make changes that may be necessary.

Are the things I do a work of faith or produced by habit?

Are my motives prompted by an attitude of love or self-gratification?

Are my thoughts focused on my hope in Christ and His return?

These are questions that bring me face to face with the reality of what life is all about.

These investments may cost me now but the dividends are "out of this world."

June 23

Sanctification

Grace and peace be yours in abundance through the knowledge of God and of Jesus our Lord.

II Peter 1:2 NIV

As believers, we want an abundance of God's grace and peace but we are not willing to spend time and effort to know Him better through prayer and meditation on His Word.

It has been said, "We don't get holy in a hurry." It is a process of growing and maturing in our faith.

No matter where we are in our spiritual journey there is always room for growth. (II Peter 3:18)

There are four things that will encourage our maturity:

> Reading Scripture
> Praying
> Fellowshipping
> Repenting

June 24

Christian Growth

*Being confident of this, that he who began a good work
in you will carry it on to completion until the day of
Christ Jesus.*
Philippians 1:6 NIV

The God who began a good work in us continues it
throughout our lifetime and will finish it when we meet
Him face to face.

God's work for us began when Christ died on the cross
in our place.

His work in us began when we first believed and
accepted Christ as our Savior and Lord.

His work through us is carried on now by the Holy
Spirit, who lives in us, enabling us to be more like
Christ each day.

We should thank God every day for what He does for
us, in us and through us for His glory.

Lord, my desire is to be where you want me to be, doing
what you want me to do, in the way you want it done.

June 25

Holiness

Since we have these promises, dear friends, let us purify ourselves from everything that contaminates body and spirit, perfecting holiness out of reverence for God.

II Corinthians 7:1 NIV

We often think that God is only concerned about our "spiritual life," and that we can separate our "life in Christ" from our daily lifestyle. This is self deception. God is concerned about our whole person—body, soul and spirit.

Our body is the vehicle of our soul and spirit. Our soul includes our mind, emotions and will. Our spirit is the dwelling place of the Holy Spirit. We are to respect our bodies as His temple and seek His will in all aspects of our life. (I Corinthians 3:16-17)

June 26

The Only Way

Jesus answered, I am the way and the truth and the life.
No one comes to the Father except through me.
John 14:6

This is one of the most basic and important passages in Scripture because it tells us how to know God and how to have a personal relationship with Him. Only through Christ can we know God. We can know about God through many different ways but we can only know Him through Christ –

> Christ is the Way to God
> Christ is the Truth about God
> Christ is the Life from God

God's purpose in sending Christ to earth was to reveal Himself to the world through Christ, and to offer Him as the perfect sacrifice to pay the penalty for man's sin.

Christ veiled (hid) His glory in human flesh, so that He could become like us. He set aside His power and strength and depended completely upon the Father. (Colossians 2:15) Christ was fully God, fully man and 100 percent innocent—the only one who could bridge the gap between man and God.

June 27

God's Love

God is love.
I John 4:16 NIV

God's nature is love. He cannot not love because love is who God is. It is His identity.

God created us to love Him and to be loved by Him. God's love is personal. Christianity is distinct from world religions because our God desires a personal relationship with every individual, fellowship and communion with each one.

God's love is unconditional. It is who He is, not just something He does. Nothing about our character or behavior can make Him love us any more or less.

God proved His love by giving his Son, Jesus, as a sacrifice to pay the penalty for our sin so we could live eternally with Him.

God's love is based on His character, not our performance.

June 28

Condemnation

*Therefore, there is now no condemnation for those who
are in Christ Jesus, because through Christ Jesus the
law of the Spirit of life set me free from the law of sin
and death.*

Romans 8:1

God sent His Son, Jesus, in the likeness of sinful man,
to be a sin offering—a substitute for man. He died in
man's place to pay the penalty for man's sin, which
was death.

The Spirit of life is the Holy Spirit. He was present at
the creation of the world and He is the power behind
the rebirth of every Christian. He gives us the power
to live the Christian life.

Daily, we must consciously choose to focus our lives on
God through prayer and reading God's Word.

We know the Holy Spirit dwells in us, not because of a
feeling but because of God's promise to those who trust
Christ for salvation. He is faithful to His promise.

June 29

Attitude of Gratitude

The Lord detests all the proud of heart. Be sure of this:
They will not go unpunished.
Proverbs 16:5 NIV

Pride goes before destruction, a haughty spirit before a fall.
Proverbs 16:18 NIV

Pride cuts off communication between God and man. God is more concerned about our attitude than He is about our actions. The proud attitude heads the list of seven things that God hates. (Proverbs 6:16-17)

God is opposed to the proud but gives grace to the humble. (James 4:6) He will not allow us to approach Him with arrogance in our heart.

There must be an attitude of submission, trust and thankfulness. Acknowledge His authority. Trust His direction. Appreciate His blessings.

June 30

God's Truth

*For who has known the mind of the Lord that he may
instruct him. But we have the mind of Christ.*
I Corinthians 2:16 NIV

God has a purpose in communicating His truth to us
and we have a responsibility to respond to His truth.
He speaks so that we are able to comprehend the truth.

He wants us to understand His message and receive it
into our mind and heart. God wants us to be conformed
to His truth—to be like Christ. Just knowing His Word
is not enough. We must live out His principles by faith.

God also wants us to communicate His truth to others.
His Word is for everyone. Not only is it life-changing for
me but as I share it with others it can be life-changing
for them also.

July

July 1

Happiness

*Blessed are those who hunger and thirst for
righteousness, for they shall be filled.*
Matthew 5:6

This is a promise from God, spoken by Jesus. Filled
with righteousness? Yes, but there are many side
effects from being filled with righteousness.

Righteousness is a gift of God's grace, in Christ, when
we accept Him as Lord. We stand before God righteous
in Christ. Through the power of the indwelling Holy
Spirit we grow in righteousness to become more like
Christ. (Romans 5:17)

As the grace of God fills our heart, there is contentment,
security, peace and hope for the future. When I am
empty of self I can know the fullness of Christ.

Jesus said this is where happiness is to be found—
knowing the fullness of Christ—me in Christ and
Christ in me. Christ is my Righteousness!

July 2

Prayer

Hear, O Lord, my righteous plea; listen to my cry. Give ear to my prayer----Psalm 17:1

When God is silent consider:

Wavering faith—doubt about God's character and faithfulness can diminish my faith and trust.

Wrong motives—God wants me to pray for His will, not my selfish desires.

Conflicts in relationships—I cannot be in tune with God unless I'm in harmony with others.

Lack of generosity—God blesses me to be an instrument of blessing.

Indifference to God's Word—God teaches us His will and His ways through His Word.

What about the times when my heart is right and His will is my desire but He still remains silent? Am I focused more on my problem than on God's person—who He is?

He will not share first place with anyone or anything.

July 3

Burdens

Cast your cares on the Lord and he will sustain you; he will never let the righteous fall.
Psalm 55:22

Burdens come from different places in various forms. They can be emotional, spiritual or physical. David often cried out to God concerning his burdens.

Some of the loads we carry are not God's plan for us. We often carry a sense of guilt after we have confessed our sin or choose to worry about the future. Then we add to that bitterness or un-forgiveness because life is not fair. The Lord will not help us carry what He has told us to release.

God does allow us to assume responsibilities that may become a burden. From His perspective, the things which are too heavy for us provide opportunities for dependence upon Him. He never intends for any of us to carry a burden without Him. Trust Him!

July 4

My Body—God's Temple

*Do not offer the parts of your body to sin, as instruments
of wickedness, but rather offer yourselves to God as
those who have been brought from death to life; and
offer the parts of your body to him as instruments of
righteousness.*
Romans 6:13 NIV

When I surrender my life to Christ, my body and soul
become His. This is a fact and to enable me to make it a
reality He indwells me in the person of His Holy Spirit.
I am to count myself as brought from death to life, to
be used by God as His instrument of righteousness.
(Romans 12:1)

I cannot rely on my own efforts to overcome the
world. Following a list of spiritual "do's" and fleshly
"don'ts" will not bring victory. Only faith in Christ
and the renewing of my mind will prepare me as God's
instrument of righteousness. (Romans 12:1-2)

July 5

Knowing God

For my thoughts are not your thoughts, neither are your ways my ways, declares the Lord.
Isaiah 55:8 NIV

One of the problems Christians have is the lack of understanding God's ways. We try to fit Him into our own ideas of how He works in and through His creation, to fulfill His purpose on earth.

Some don't believe that God works miracles at all, while others are convinced that if he is not doing the miraculous He is not at work. We forget that God is Sovereign over His creation—He can do what He chooses, how He chooses, when He chooses.

We need a balanced perspective which we can find in the Bible. God works in both supernatural and ordinary ways. Seeing the work of God in miracles is easy, but He is just as involved in the common place aspects of life as He is in the supernatural events.

Look for His "fingerprint" in your daily activities, directing your path.

July 6

Faith and Obedience

The word of the Lord came to Elijah: Go and present
yourself to Ahab, and I will send rain on the land. So
Elijah went to present himself to Ahab.
I Kings 18-1-2

Faith and obedience travel hand in hand. Faith encourages obedience and obedience strengthens faith. As they are practiced each grows in its own special way. We believe God, therefore we obey Him. When we obey God He encourages us in our faith in Christ.

Fear short-circuits faith and opens our mind to doubt God and His Word. Satan uses our fear and disobedience to hinder us in the plans God has for our life.

Great faith begins with small steps. When we choose to believe God's Word, step out on faith in obedience to Him, an ever increasing cycle begins—faith, trust, obedience.

Believe God!

July 7

Prayer

The eyes of the Lord are on the righteous, and his ears are open to their prayers.
I Peter 3:12

It is not easy to shut out the world and set aside some moments to spend with the Lord in God's Word and prayer. But it is essential if we want to grow in our relationship with Him.

I have learned that you don't find time - you take time.

Many are faced with the temptation to get so busy working for the Lord that they don't spend time with Him. Our intimacy with Him grows as we spend quiet time with Him, meditating on His Word which describes his character and nature.

He tells us to "Be still and know that I am God." (Psalm 46:10) God desires to make His presence, His protection, His provisions, His power real in our daily life.

When we get so caught up in the ways of the world we may know Him in our head but miss Him in our heart.

July 8

Triumphant Living

*Walk in all the way that the Lord your God has
commanded you, so that you may live and prosper and
prolong your days in the land that you will possess.*

Deuteronomy 5:33 NIV

The world thinks of the good life as being based on
wealth, fame and position. When we consider the facts
of life today we know that these achievements do not
always bring success and happiness. True success
means becoming the person God has called us to be
and reaching the goals He has planned for us.

God wrote the book on triumphant living. He has
recorded His principles in His Word, The Bible. He
has given us examples, along with consequences for
disobedience and rewards for obedience.

The only way to live victoriously is God's Way. Living
the good life means joy, peace and contentment.

July 9

Guilt

If we confess our sins, he is faithful and just and will forgive us our sins and purify us from all unrighteousness.

I John 1:9

When we accept Christ as our substitute in death, to pay the penalty for our sin, He forgives all the sins we have committed or will ever commit. Our relationship is secure in Christ. As Christians, when we sin, we are to confess and repent of our sins so we can enjoy fellowship with Christ daily.

One of Satan's subtle ways of hindering our walk with the Lord is to influence us with a sense of guilt and condemnation. Guilt leads to doubt of God's love and salvation, which paves the way for fear, insecurity and inability to enjoy life. It can also lead to depression.

There are two types of guilt—biblical and false. Biblical guilt is from the violation of a scriptural law. It is not a feeling but a reality; we have sinned and should repent.

False guilt is feeling guilty after confessing a sin. It is not based on truth supported by the Word.

Satan wants us to forget the unconfessed sins and remember those we have confessed and been forgiven.

Reject him in the Name of Jesus, and any sense of guilt.

July 10

The Kingdom of God

He appeared to them over a period of forty days and
spoke about the kingdom of God.
Acts 1:3b NIV

Jesus explained that with His coming, the kingdom of God was inaugurated. When He returned to heaven, God's kingdom would remain in the hearts of all believers through the presence of the Holy Spirit. But the kingdom of God will not be fully realized until Jesus Christ comes again to judge all people and remove all evil from the world.

During the years of Jesus' ministry on earth, the disciples continually wondered about His kingdom. The traditional view: The Messiah would be an earthly king who would free Israel from Rome. But the kingdom Jesus spoke about was first of all a spiritual kingdom established in the hearts and lives of individual believers. (Luke 17:21) God's presence and power indwells believers in the person of the Holy Spirit.

July 11

God's Timing

He said to them: It is not for you to know the times or dates the Father has set by his own authority.

Acts 1:7

Jesus said that God the Father sets the timetable for all events—worldwide, national and personal. If you want changes that God isn't making immediately, don't become impatient. Instead, trust God's timetable.

History is not haphazard or cyclical; it is moving toward a specific point—the return of Jesus to judge and rule over the earth. We should be ready for His sudden return. (I Thessalonians 5:2)

After Jesus' resurrection He returned to heaven bodily and visibly and one day He will return to earth in the same way. (Acts 1:11)

July 12

Peace with God

*Therefore, since we have been justified through faith, we
have peace with God through our Lord Jesus Christ.*
Romans 5:1 NIV

Peace with God means that we have been reconciled
with Him. There is no more hostility between us, no
sin blocking our relationship with Him. Peace with
God is possible only because Jesus paid the price for
our sins, through His death on the cross.

We enjoy the peace that comes by being made right
with God but we still face daily problems. The problems
often help us grow. As God's children we are recipients
of His grace—He protects and provides for us.

The heart of the Christian life is faith, hope and love.
It begins with faith, grows through hope and reaches
out in love to others.

July 13

Responsibility

*For the lips of the priest ought to preserve knowledge,
and from his mouth men should seek instruction—
because he is the messenger of the Lord Almighty.*
Malachi 2:7

Pastors, leaders and teachers of God's people must know God's word—what it says, what it means and how it applies to daily life. Know the interpretation and recognize the applications.

There should be no partiality in confronting sin and dealing with it. Too many people want to hear a message that will "tickle their ears," and make them feel comfortable.

Malachi's message concerned a people who were unfaithful—not in word but in action. They lived as though they could do anything without being punished.

God is "Lord of all" or He is not Lord at all.

July 14

Training Our Children

Train a child in the way he should go, and when he is old he will not turn from it.
Proverbs 22:6

Start a child in the way he should go and keep him headed in that direction (my paraphrase). From the beginning parents should discern the individuality and special strengths God has given each child. This is the "way he should go." We have desires and plans for our children and we try to fit them into those plans.

God has created us as unique individuals. Each child has natural inclinations that parents can develop. Many parents want to make all the choices for their child; but it's important to teach a child how to make decisions. Train them to choose the right way. How?

    1) Invest time in their lives.
    2) Listen closely (know what they are thinking).
    3) Protect through discipline, in love.
    4) Be transparent, admit own mistakes.
    5) Express unconditional love.

Teach your children that they are accountable to God, as well as parents, for their decisions.

July 15

Doubt

*If any of you lacks wisdom, he should ask God, who
gives generously to all without finding fault, and it will
be given to him. But when he asks, he must believe and
not doubt.*

James 1:5

Doubt started in the Garden of Eden when Satan
deceived Eve and he is still whispering lies to Christians
today. The wisdom James is referring to is the ability
to make wise decisions in difficult situations or
circumstances. We can ask for God's wisdom to guide
our choices.

Wisdom means practical discernment. It begins with
respect for God, leads to right living and the ability to
tell right from wrong.

To "believe and not doubt," means believing in the
existence of God but also relying on Him and expecting
Him to hear and answer when we pray.

July 16

Heaven

Now we know that if the earthly tent (this body we live in) is destroyed, we have an eternal house in heaven, not built by human hands.
II Corinthians 5:1 NIV

Death is our passport from life on earth to eternity. For the Christian, "to be absent from the body is to be present with the Lord." (v. 6-8) The Holy Spirit, indwelling the believer, is our guarantee, a deposit on what is to come. (v. 5)

Jesus is preparing our dwelling place to be with Him. Our tent (body) will be like His, an eternal body that will be suitable for our eternal life. God created us for this purpose.

Jesus died to fulfill God's plan of redemption, not just for the soul but also for the body.

I can choose to accept Jesus, as my substitute in death for sin, and spend eternity with Him, or reject Him and spend eternity separated from God.

"If I die daily my final day will be no problem. Death will be preparation for another day."

July 17

Faith

Then he said, Jesus, remember me when you come into your kingdom.

Jesus answered him, I tell you the truth, today you will be with me in paradise.

Luke 23:42-43 NIV

Three men died on crosses the day Jesus was crucified. One man died in his sin, one man died for sin and the other died to sin. Two men were guilty under law and being punished as deserved. One man was innocent, dying as a substitute for the guilty.

The two who were guilty had the same opportunity to accept the substitute as his Savior. One accepted, by faith, what Jesus said. His destiny was changed to Paradise and eternity with Jesus.

The other rejected the truth and his destiny was settled—separation from Christ for eternity.

Jesus said, "I am the Way, the Truth and the Life." Trust Him!

July 18

Salvation

In reply Jesus declared, I tell you the truth, no one can see the kingdom of God unless he is born again.
John 3:3

The expression, "born again Christian," was popular several years ago. This was really a misnomer because the real definition of a Christian is one who has "been born again," (born from above) as Jesus explained the new birth to Nicodemus. Believers were given the name Christian to describe them as "followers of Christ."

Believers need to be aware that some of the expressions (words and phrases) that we use can be confusing for unbelievers. As witnesses, we need to be discerning as we share the truth of God's Word.

Sometimes we refer to people as being "lost" or "saved." What do we mean?

Lost—No relationship with God through Jesus Christ. (Separation from God)

Saved—A personal relationship with God through spiritual rebirth.

John 1:13
>Who were born, not of blood, nor of the will of the flesh, nor of the will of man, but of God.

July 19

God's Love

This is how God showed his love among us: he sent his one and only Son into the world that we might live through him. This is love: not that we loved God, but that he loved us and sent his Son as an atoning sacrifice for our sins.

I John 4:9-10 NIV

Love explains:

1) Why God creates—because He loves, He creates people to love.

2) Why God cares—because He loves them He cares for sinful people.

3) Why we are free to choose—God wants a loving response from us.

4) Why Christ died—His love for us caused Him to seek a solution to the problem of sin.

5) Why we receive eternal life—God's love expresses itself to us forever.

God sent Jesus to die for us, not because we were good enough but because He loved us.
(Romans 5:8)

July 20

Success

*Be strong and very courageous. Be careful to obey the law my
servant Moses gave you; do not turn from it to the right or to
the left, that you may be successful wherever you go. Do not
let this Book of the Law depart from your mouth; meditate on
it day and night, so that you may be careful to do everything
written in it. Then you will be prosperous and successful.*
Joshua 1:7-8 NIV

This is "God's principle for success."

The world's principle: "Fame + Fortune = Success."

God's principle: "Be strong and courageous + obey
God's law + study God's Word = Success."

Psalm 1:1   Blessed is the man ---(v. 2) whose delight is
in the law of the Lord, and on his law he meditates day
and night ---whatever he does prospers.

Don't miss this: God may have planned, promised and
provided but our personal success has some conditions.
God will not violate our will. We are free to make
choices but not free to determine the consequences.
This is God's choice.

We are to:
1)   Establish God-given goals. He has recorded
     His principles in His Word to direct us.
2)   Obey His principles. He has promised to
     reward our obedience.
3)   Rely upon the Holy Spirit. He has provided a
     Teacher and Helper in the person of His Holy
     Spirit.
Our daily prayer should be –
Lord, I want to be where you want me to be, doing what
you want me to do, the way you want me to do it.

July 21

The Greatest Commandment

Hear, O Israel: The Lord our God, the Lord is one. Love the Lord your God with all your heart and with all your soul and with all your strength.
Deuteronomy 6:4-5 NIV

Through Moses, God was instructing His people to love Him with all of their being. God created man as body, soul and spirit. The body is the vehicle of the soul and spirit; the dwelling place of the Holy Spirit, in the believer. (I Corinthians 6:19)

Our body is the physical strength of our being. God is pleased when we treat it with respect; we are loving Him with our strength.

Our soul involves our mind (intellect), emotions (feelings), and, our will (desires). It is an expression of our personality. Through our soul we relate to ourselves and others.

In our spirit (heart) we relate to God our Creator, the source of our being, who gave us our individuality.

All of our being is to be involved in our expression of love to God.

This is true worship. All that I am delighting in all that God is.

July 22

Filled With The Spirit

Do not get drunk on wine, which leads to debauchery.
Instead, be filled with the Spirit.
Ephesians 5:18

Christians are indwelt and sealed by the Holy Spirit when they accept Christ as Savior. Being filled with the Spirit (controlled by Him) is a choice. He will not override our will but waits for us to choose His leading.

God wants us to desire His fullness and He uses different methods to accomplish His purpose. Sometimes He places a longing in our heart to be close to Him. At other times He uses our sense of failure from trying to live in our own strength. God even uses the example of other people, who are Spirit-filled, to cause the desire in our heart.

Being filled with the Spirit is a progressive lifestyle—a gradual peeling away of layers of self-rule, a discipline of denying self.

July 23

Rest in the Lord

*Come to me, all you who are weary and burdened, and
I will give you rest. Take my yoke upon you and learn
from me, for I am gentle and humble in heart, and you
will find rest for your souls. For my yoke is easy and my
burden is light.*
Matthew 11:28-30 NIV

When stress and problems weigh us down the most
natural response is to ask God for relief. "Lord, I can't
carry this anymore. I'm going to leave it with you."
Then we walk away but remain unchanged inside.
This is not how God works.

Christ's invitation is to join Him in the yoke so we
can walk and work together. He doesn't just want
the burden, He wants me. The yoke is a symbol of
discipleship which includes submission and obedience
to Him.

The process of lightening the load begins with learning
to know and understand the Lord. The burden is not
necessarily removed but my thoughts and responses
are changed as I begin to love Him, trust Him, believe
His promises and rely on His power. As the weight
shifts from my shoulders to His I am relieved even
though the situation may not change.

July 24

Alone With God

Be still and know that I am God.
Psalm 46:10

Our Father doesn't speak to us in the same exact manner as He spoke with the Old Testament prophets, but the process of receiving the message hasn't changed. It begins with being alone in His presence and involves listening as He speaks through His Word. But it shouldn't end there. We are to share with others what we learn from God's Word. Devotional time with the Lord is not just about our own interests and needs. The Father reveals His treasures to us so we can share them with others.

Spend time each day with God in His Word and prayer. Believe what He says in Scripture, and apply it to your life, then share with someone else what He has revealed. The authority of your message comes from Him.

Our prayer and Bible study becomes a time of fellowship and communion with the Father. As a result we grow in our identification with Christ through which we come to know God in a more intimate way.

July 25

Letting Go

But whatever was to my profit I now consider loss for the sake of Christ.
Philippians 3:7

Life is more than "stuff." Stuff doesn't last—life does! It has been said, "One person's junk is another person's treasure."

I've always had a problem "getting rid" of things I never use—items that are tied to family, friends and important events. It's like throwing away part of my life. I remember how I struggled with disposing of my parents personal belongings. I realize that I need to make those decisions now and spare my children of that responsibility, but I haven't done it yet.

It's true, that given time, my trophies will be trashed by someone else.

Lord, give me grace to let go now.

Speak to us, Lord, 'til shamed by Thy great giving,
Our hands unclasp to set our treasures free;
Our wills, our love, our dear ones, our possessions,
All gladly yielded, gracious Lord, to Thee.

Amen

July 26

Heart

Create in me a pure heart, O God, and renew a steadfast spirit within me. Psalm 51:10 NIV

I will give you a new heart and put a new spirit in you; I will remove from you your heart of stone and give you a heart of flesh. Ezekiel 36:26 NIV

God has much to say about the heart, in His Word. He describes it as sinful, clean, pure, whole, divided, upright, sincere, free, determined, obedient, blameless, joyful, perfect, proud, merry, stoney and etc.

Psalm 51 is a prayer of confession and repentance by David. He acknowledges his sin as being against God, although others were involved too. All sin is against God first and foremost and must be confessed to Him. He then forgives and cleanses the heart.

God referred to David as a man "after His own heart," because he always sought God's forgiveness when he sinned. He had a soft, pliable heart that God could remold.

> Lord, my desire is to be like you,
> Encouraging in what I say;
> An example in what I do.
> Your glory, not mine, I seek to display,
> As I walk with you,
> Throughout this day.

July 27

Faith

Nothing can hinder the Lord from saving, whether by many or by few.
I Samuel 14:6b NIV

Trusting the Lord is a process, which must be learned through experience. Sometimes God places us in situations that we see as impossible. When He takes us through it our faith is strengthened and we are encouraged in His faithfulness.

The Lord delights in demonstrating His awesome power and glory through our weakness and inadequacy. Seek His will and obey Him—leave the consequences to God Almighty.

> You give me strength day by day,
> You encourage me along the way.
> You provide for every need,
> When I lose my way, you're there to lead.
>
> I'll rest in the promise of your presence,
> For you are faithful and true.
> It is written in your Eternal Word,
> "I'll never leave nor forsake you."

July 28

Faith

For in the gospel a righteousness from God is revealed, a righteousness that is by faith from first to last, just as it is written: The righteous shall live by faith.

Romans 1:17 NIV

We must be careful to understand faith as Paul uses the word because he ties faith so closely to salvation. We often hear someone say, "we're saved by faith." Faith is not something we must do in order to earn salvation. We are saved by grace through faith—by God's grace through God's faith, a gift He gives us because He is saving us. (Ephesians 2:8)

We can never come to God through our own faith. When we accept the gift of God's grace he plants the seed of faith within us.

He encourages us in that faith through His Word, prayer, people and circumstances so that we learn to live by faith. Walking by faith is a lifestyle, a way in which we conduct ourselves.

July 29

Peace

*Peace I leave with you; my peace I give you. I do not give
you as the world gives. Do not let your heart be troubled
and do not be afraid.*

John 14:27 NIV

The world defines peace as "the absence of conflict."
God's peace is "confident assurance" in any
circumstances. With God's peace we have no need to
fear the present or the future.

God gives us a wonderful promise in Philippians 4:6, 7,
concerning His peace. Only God's peace can comfort
our heart in this world of sin, fear, doubt, conflict and
stress. As we read and meditate upon God's Word, and
seek His will through prayer, the Holy Spirit will plant
God's truth in our mind. As we face a troubled world
the Holy Spirit will remind us of God's faithfulness.

> Peace! God's wonderful peace,
> Filling my heart, removing the fear.
> Renewing my mind, at rest in Him,
> Knowing His love and presence near.

July 30

Faith

What does the Lord your God ask of you but to fear the Lord your God, to walk in all his ways, to love him, to serve the Lord your God with all your heart and with all your soul, and to observe the Lord's commands and decrees. Deuteronomy 19: 12, 13

We often ask ourselves, "What does God expect of me?"

Moses gives a summary to Israel that is easy to remember. The essentials:

> Fear God (have reverence for Him)
> Walk in all His ways
> Love Him
> Serve Him with all your heart and soul
> Observe His commands

Do you have a deep desire to please God?
Concentrate on His real requirements:

> Respect, follow, love, serve, obey.

The Bible portrays the Christian life as a walk. It speaks of walking in the Spirit, in God's ways, in love and in truth.

> Focus on God's promises, presence and peace.

July 31

Who is Jesus?

But what about you? he asked. Who do you say I am?
Matthew 16:15 NIV

Every person will have to answer this question at sometime. (Romans 14:11) We can choose when we will answer, whether here on earth or in eternity. The place and time will determine the consequences, and your destiny. Eternal Life or Eternal Death.

The Scriptures tell us who Jesus is. (John 5:39) Once we have that information, we must decide what to do with it. We either accept or reject Jesus as Savior. To avoid the question is actually a form of rejection. (John 3:18)

1) Jesus is God's Son. (Matthew 3:17)
2) Jesus is the Savior of Mankind. (II Corinthians 5:21)
3) Jesus is our High Priest. (Hebrews 4:15; 7:26)

The only mediator between God and man. Jesus said to him, I am the way, and the truth, and the life; no one comes to the Father but through me." (John 14:6 NASB)

When we know Jesus Christ as our personal Savior, we are to share Him with others. (Matthew 18:19-20)

August

August 1

Hospitality

Offer hospitality to one another without grumbling.
I Peter 4:9 NIV

Hospitality simply means making other people feel comfortable and at home.

Christian hospitality differs from social entertaining. Entertaining focuses on the host—the home must be spotless, food must be well prepared and abundant, the host must appear relaxed and good natured. Hospitality by contrast, focuses on the guest. Their needs—whether for a place to stay, nourishing food, a listening ear, or acceptance—are the primary concern.

Hospitality can happen in a messy home. It can happen around a dinner table where the main dish is canned soup. It can even happen while the host and guest are doing chores together. Don't hesitate to offer hospitality just because you're too tired, too busy or not wealthy enough to entertain.

Your possessions, status and power will mean nothing in God's kingdom, but you will spend eternity with other people. Invest your time and talents where they will make an eternal difference.

Our Walk

*Now when Abram was ninety-nine years old, the
Lord appeared to Abram and said to him, "I am God
Almighty; walk before me, and be blameless."*
Genesis 17:1 NASB

God revealed Himself to Abraham as El Shaddai, God
Almighty, the One who can supply every need.

To "walk before" suggests a child running ahead and
playing in the presence of his father, conscious of his
perfect security because his father is near.

The children of Israel were told to "walk after" the Lord
and keep His commandments. (Deuteronomy 13:4)

To "walk after" pictures a servant following his master.

It is written that Enoch and Noah "walked with God."
(Genesis 5:24; 6:9)

To "walk with" God indicates fellowship and friendship.

For those who are members of the Body of Christ, we
are told to "walk in" Him. (Colossians 2:6)

To "walk in" symbolizes union.

Christians are to "walk before" God as children—
trusting Him. We are to "walk after" Him—serving. We
are to "walk with" Him—in fellowship and communion.
We "walk in" Him as members of His body.

This is what Paul had in mind when he said, "Walk by
the Spirit." (Galatians 5:16)

God's Will

When they came to the border of Mysia, they tried to enter Bithynia, but the Spirit of Jesus would not allow them to.

Acts 16:7

To know God's will does not mean we must hear His voice. He leads in different ways.

When seeking God's will, (1) make sure your plan is in harmony with God's Word; (2) ask mature Christians for their advice; (3) check your motives—are you seeking what you want or what God wants? (4) pray for God to open and close doors as He desires.

As we seek God's will, it is important to know what God wants us to do and where He wants us to go, but it is just as important to know what He does not want us to do and where He does not want us to go.

The Lord will make a straight path for us when we choose to trust Him rather than self. (Proverbs 3:5-6)

When one door is closed a greater one is about to open. Watch for it. Don't be afraid for God to correct your plans. He'll give you wisdom if you are willing to wait and listen.

August 4

Preparation for Prayer

With all prayer and petition pray at all times in the
Spirit, and with this in view, be on the alert with all
perseverance and petition for all the saints.
Ephesians 6:18

Praise God for His Greatness –

Acknowledge His presence, His power, His knowledge and wisdom, mindful of our dependence upon Him. Be sensitive to the Holy Spirit's prompting, as He leads, in our thoughts and desires.

As He convicts of sins that will hinder our prayers from being answered, confess those sins, repent, and claim forgiveness and cleansing through the blood of Jesus.

Ask God for wisdom and discernment as you seek the mind of Christ in praying for individuals, situations and needs that you have, as the Holy Spirit brings them to your mind.

Always be mindful of God's love and goodness and His desire to share His goodness as an expression of His love while working for you, in you and through you to glorify Himself.

His ultimate purpose is for us to be where He wants us to be, doing what He wants us to do, the way He wants us to do it.

Eternal Security

For God so loved the world that he gave his one and only Son, that whosoever believes in him shall not perish but have eternal life. John 3:16

If you believe that Jesus Christ is the Son of God and that His death on the cross purchased God's forgiveness for your sins, then you are saved and you can be sure.

God's promises never change. He said that those who trust in His Son would have eternal life. (John 5:24) A believer cannot be snatched from God's hand. (John 10:29-30)

The Lord loves us unconditionally. Nothing can separate a believer from God's love. (Romans 8:35-29) The Savior's work on the cross is finished. Jesus made one perfect sacrifice His own life. In this single act, He paid for every sinful deed, thought, word. (Hebrews 9:11-12, 26)

When we receive His Salvation it is ours forever. The Lord revealed His character through the cross:

Unconditional love—dying for those who sinned against Him.

Righteousness—the perfect sacrifice, sinless, paid the penalty.

Faithfulness—redeeming Savior of mankind.

Power—conquered sin and death, eternal security.

Assurance for today—security for tomorrow. We don't have to know the future to have faith in God; we have to have faith in God to be secure about the future.

August 6

Sin

The death he died, he died to sin once for all; but the life he lives, he lives to God. In the same way, count yourselves dead to sin but alive to God in Christ Jesus. Therefore, do not let sin reign in your mortal body so that you obey its evil desires.

Romans 6:10-12

Being dead to sin means that I consider my old sinful nature as dead and unresponsive to sin. I no longer have to live by my old motives and desires. In Christ, I can overcome the old nature by the power of the Holy Spirit indwelling me. I can become all that Christ has declared me to be in Him.

A recurring pattern of wrongdoing indicates captivity to sin.

How can I deal with it?

Recognize and admit the problem.

Choose to make a change.

Believe God's promise that He can and will enable me to change.

Exercise faith in who Christ is and who I am in Him.

Financial Security

But seek first his kingdom and his righteousness, and
all these things will be given to you as well.
Matthew 6:33

To "seek first His kingdom and His righteousness" means to turn to God first. Think about His desires, His promises and His character.

The Lord is not too busy to be concerned about our financial situation. He cares about every detail of our life. Financial security is not found in bank accounts or retirement funds but in a relationship with the one who owns everything in heaven and on earth. When we follow His direction about money we will experience joy, peace and contentment.

Three basic truths to consider:

1) God owns it all.

2) We are managers of His possessions.

3) We will one day give an account to Him about the way we used His resources.

August 8

Faith

I tell you the truth, anyone who will not receive the kingdom of God like a little child will never enter it.
Mark 10:15

All a little child needs to be happy and secure is a loving look and a gentle touch from someone who cares. They believe anyone that they trust.

Verse 16 says, "And he took the children in his arms, put his hands on them and blessed them."

Jesus is saying, "The Father wants our simple faith and trust in Him. We don't have to understand all the mysteries and details of the universe. It should be enough to know God loves us and provides forgiveness for our sins.

God is a gentle Father who meets us where we are but doesn't leave us there. He continues to fill our heart with a yearning and sense of need for Jesus. His arm about us and His hand upon us is our security in this life and eternity.

Prayer

Let us then approach the throne of grace with confidence,
so that we may receive mercy and find grace to help us in
our time of need. Hebrews 4:16

The way to handle life's troubles is discovered through prayer. Our heavenly Father waits for us to approach His throne to gain His perspective, and receive instruction on how to proceed.

He knows all things and is all-powerful. He can soften hard hearts, open closed minds and change attitudes.

We are to come in reverence because our God is Holy but we can come with bold assurance because He is our Friend.

When praying the condition of the heart is more important than the position of the body.

"Joy Stealers"

Worry –An anxiety about something that may or may not happen. (Usually doesn't)
　　　　Pray—let go and let God.

Stress—Intense strain over a situation we can't change or control. (But God can)
　　　　Rest—wait on God

Fear —Dreadful uneasiness over danger, evil or pain. (It magnifies our problems)

　　　　　　Faith—trust in God.
　　　　　　He is faithful to His promise!

August 10

Prayer

Devote yourselves to prayer, being watchful and thankful.

Colossians 4:2

Have you ever grown tired of praying for something or someone?

Our persistence is an expression of our faith that God answers our prayers.

God's delays may be His way of working His will in our lives. We only see the obvious but God sees behind the scene—hearts, minds, motives, and attitudes that need to be changed. God's timing is not always based on our thinking but on what He knows is best in each situation.,

Our responsibility is to pray and watch how He works in lives to bring about what is best and be thankful for what He does.

God's ultimate desire for His children is not happiness but holiness and He works in our lives daily to fulfill that desire.

August 11

Faith

So do not fear, for I am with you; do not be dismayed,
for I am your God. I will strengthen you and help you; I
will uphold you with my righteous right hand.
Isaiah 41:10 NIV

At a time in my life, when I was experiencing great physical pain, the Lord brought this verse to my mind and I have often claimed it when going through difficult times.

In verse 13 God says again "For I am the Lord your God who takes hold of your right hand and says to you, 'Do not fear I will help you.'"

We need not fear for (1) God is with us ("I am with you"); (2) God has established a relationship with us, ("I am your God"); and, (3) God gives us assurance of His strength, help and victory over sin and death.

He is never too tired or too busy to help and listen. His strength is our source of strength. Call upon Him!

August 12

Grace

But to each one of us grace has been given as Christ
apportioned it. Ephesians 4:7

Each believer has God-given abilities that can strengthen the whole body. Your ability may seem large or small but it is yours to use in service.

Healthy self-esteem is important because some of us think too little of ourselves; on the other hand, some of us overestimate ourselves. The key to an honest evaluation is knowing the basis of our self-worth—our identity in Christ. Apart from Him we are not capable of very much.

God gives us gifts so we can build up His church. To use them effectively, we must (1) realize that all gifts and abilities come from God; (2) understand that not everyone has the same gifts; (3) know who we are and what we do best; (4) dedicate our gifts to God and not serve out of personal success; and, (5) be willing to exercise our gifts wholeheartedly.

God's gifts differ in nature, power and effectiveness according to His wisdom and graciousness, not according to our faith. The "measure of faith" means God will give spiritual power necessary to carry out each responsibility. These are God's gifts to His church and He gives faith and power as He wills. Our role is to be faithful.

August 13

Guidance

*Show me your way, O Lord, teach me your path; guide
me in your truth and teach me, for you are God my
Savior, and my hope is in you all day long.*
Psalm 25:4-5

As a shepherd, David spent much of his time meditating. Meditating is not something we spend a lot of time on today. There are too many other things claiming our time. If we sincerely desire to know God—His will, His ways and His work—it is vital that we spend time with Him and it involves meditating on His Word.

When we are willing to seek God, learn from His Word and obey His commands, then we can receive specific guidance.

The first step is to want to be guided and to realize that guidance comes from His Word. Psalm 119 tells of the endless knowledge to be found in God's Word.

Lord, as I read your Word day by day,
May I hide it in my heart and obey –
So others can see in my walk and way,
That I truly practice what I say.

August 14

Words

Let no unwholesome word proceed from your mouth, but only such a word as is good for edification according to the need of the moment, so that it will give grace to those who hear.

Ephesians 4:29 NASB

The old saying, "Sticks and stones may break my bones but words can never hurt me," is not true. Emotional feelings are sometimes more sensitive than physical hurt and can take longer to heal.

The words we speak, whether to one person or many, can spread like wild fire. James tells us the tongue is a restless evil, full of deadly poison. (James 3:8)

What we say and what we don't say are both important. God's Word has warnings about the words we use. (Gossip?)

Proverbs 25:11—
A word fitly spoken is like apples of gold
in pictures of silver.

Worry

*Therefore do not worry about tomorrow, for tomorrow
will worry about itself. Each day has enough trouble of
its own.*
Matthew 6:34 NIV

God created man with the ability to trust Him in all
things. God had provided everything man needed even
before He created man. It didn't take man long to
transfer that trust to himself.

Man soon learned that he could not trust himself. No
longer could he do what was right or keep from doing
what was wrong. The result—worry—could God be
trusted?

Because of the negative effect of worry on our physical,
emotional, mental and spiritual life, Jesus tells us not
to worry about the things God has promised to supply.
We are to seek God and His righteousness, first,
trusting Him to guide us in our choices.

Don't let worries about tomorrow hinder your
fellowship with God today. (Philippians 4:6-7)

August 16

Faith

Consider it pure joy my brothers whenever you face trials of many kinds, because you know that the testing of your faith develops perseverance. Perseverance must finish its work so that you may be mature and complete, not lacking anything.
James 1:2-4

None of us seek to go through pain and suffering but James tells us it may be necessary to test our faith. The experience can be a way of spiritual growth and maturity.

The Creation of a Pearl

The oyster produces a pearl as a result of irritation when the shell of an oyster is invaded by an alien substance—like a grain of sand. When that happens, all of the resources within the tiny sensitive oyster rush to the irritated spot and begin to release healing fluids that otherwise would remain dormant. By and by, the irritation is covered and turns into a beautiful pearl. Had there been no irritating interruption, there could have been no pearl.

August 17

The Word

*How can a young man keep his way pure? By living
according to your word.*
Psalm 1219:9 NIV

In an effort to live a life that is pleasing to the Lord, we
can easily get so caught up in doing work for the Lord,
that we forget what our relationship with God is all
about. We forget the basics—prayer and Bible study—
and in our busyness to serve the Lord we actually
drift farther from Him. Our first priority should be
fellowship and communion with God and as a result of
that experience we are prepared to serve Him.

The value of God's Word cannot be measured. Not only
is the Bible our guide, by which to live our lives, it also
shows us the way to our heavenly Father's heart. It all
begins with a desire to do what His Word says in every
circumstance and when that becomes our lifestyle our
way will be pure.

August 18

The Word

*I have hidden your Word in my heart that I might not
sin against you.*
Psalm 119:11

The only way we can hide God's Word in our heart
is to read, meditate and reflect upon it day by day.
It is a process of renewing my mind to think godly
thoughts and to see from His perspective. We grow
in the knowledge of His will and the way He works to
accomplish His will.

When we are faced with temptations the Holy Spirit
can bring to our mind the scripture that can apply to
that sin and enable us to resist the temptation.

God is faithful; He will not let you be tempted beyond
what you can bear. But when you are tempted, He will
also provide a way out so that you can stand up under
it. (I Corinthians 10:13)

Choices

But if serving the Lord seems undesirable to you, then choose for yourselves this day whom you will serve.
Joshua 24:15a NIV

Life is made up of choices. Each day we are faced with new ones—some are more important than others.

Many things in life we do not have the opportunity to choose—the weather, the economy, etc. I had no choice about my parents, my physical features, or about how people respond to me. I do have a choice about the most important thing in my life—my destiny—my relationship with God and where I will spend eternity. God has given me that choice.

The way has been made plain, in His Word, and the consequences if I make the wrong choice.

Jesus made the first choice—to die for me—without His choice I would have no choice.

Thank you Lord!

August 20

The Evil One (Prayer)

The Lord is faithful, and he will strengthen and protect you from the evil one.
II Thessalonians 3:3

Beneath the surface of the routine of daily living, a fierce struggle among invisible spiritual powers is being waged. Our main defense is prayer that God will protect us from the evil one and that He will strengthen us

Guidelines to help you prepare and survive Satan's attacks:

1) Take the threat of spiritual attack seriously.
2) Pray for strength and help from God.
3) Study the Bible to recognize Satan's subtle style and tactics.
4) Memorize Scripture so it will be a source of help.
5) Associate with those who know and speak the truth.
6) Practice what you are taught by spiritual leaders.

An Evening Prayer

Lord, it's been a wonderful day.
Thank you for the blessings you sent my way;
Your presence to lead where I need to go,
Your word to each what I need to know.
For contact with friends and family away;
Especially with You as I knelt to pray.
As I close my eyes for rest and sleep;
Safe from the "evil one," I trust You'll keep.

Living By Faith

So then just as you received Jesus Christ as Lord,
continue to live in him, strengthened in the faith as you
were taught, and overflowing with thankfulness.

Colossians 2:6-7

We accept Christ as Lord, initially, in faith with thanksgiving, rejoicing in that experience. Paul says we should continue our Christian life in the same way, day by day.

It doesn't always happen that way. Many find ourselves drifting back into our former ways. Our joy is soon overshadowed with the cares of the world.

Solutions to hinder drifting:

1) Concentration on the Word of God.

   We become "firmly rooted" in Christ as we practice the presence and principles of Christ. Regular reading, studying and meditating on the Word of God will build Christlike character into our lives.

2) A focus on praise and worship.
   Recognizing our dependence upon God. His unconditional love and power expressed in our life daily.

3) Love and concern for others.
   Service and fellowship with other Christians.

August 22

Faith

For it is by grace you have been saved, through faith—
and this not from yourselves, it is the gift of God—not by
works, so that no one can boast.
Ephesians 2:8-9

Often we hear someone say, "We're saved by faith." That statement can be misunderstood. We're saved "by grace," through faith. It is the object of our faith, Jesus Christ, who saves us, not our emotional intensity.

Biblical faith is simple trust in the faithfulness and power of God. It is God's grace that enables us to exercise faith in Christ. Salvation is a work of God in our life, from beginning to the end. That is why it is so amazing!

Since our performance could not change our sinful condition or our eternal destiny, neither can it alter our eternal security. Our behavior, while affecting our fellowship and fruitfulness, can never diminish our security.

Holy Living

*Since then you have been raised with Christ, set your
hearts on things above, where Christ is seated at the
right hand of God. Set your minds on things above, not
on earthy things.*
Colossians 2:1-2 NIV

Let the peace of Christ rule in your hearts—Let the
word of Christ dwell in you richly—Colossians 3:15a,
16a NIV

Paul's admonition to us is to set and let.

Setting our hearts on things above means focusing on
heaven's priorities, in our daily life.

Setting our minds on things above means concentrating
on the eternal rather than the temporal. Look at life
from God's perspective and seek what He desires. We
must not become too attached to what is temporary.

When we allow the peace of Christ to rule in our hearts
we can live in peace with others. This is a choice we
can make as the Holy Spirit does His work in our life,
producing peace and love.

The Word of Christ can dwell in us as we read, meditate
and pray through God's Word daily and obey it as the
Holy Spirit makes application in our life.

August 24

The Word

Your word, O Lord, is eternal; it stands firm in the heavens. Psalm 119:8-9 NIV

Psalm 18:7-11

> The law of the Lord is perfect, reviving the soul.
> The statues of the Lord are trustworthy, making wise the simple.
> The precepts of the Lord are right, giving joy to the heart.
> The commands of the Lord are radiant, giving light to the eyes.
> The fear of the Lord is pure, enduring forever.
> The ordinances of the Lord are sure and altogether righteous.
> They are more precious than gold, than much pure gold.
> They are sweeter than honey, than honey from the comb.
> By them is your servant warned; in keeping them is great reward.

When we think of the law we think of something binding, that keeps us from having fun. But here we see God's law as freeing us to enjoy life.

God's laws are guidelines and light for our paths. They point out danger to protect us and promises to direct us.

August 25

Prayer

*And I pray that now at last, by God's will, the way may
be opened for me to come to you.*
Romans 1:10

When you pray continually about a concern don't be
surprised at how God answers. Paul prayed to visit
Rome so he could teach the Christians there. When he
finally arrived in Rome, he was a prisoner. (Acts 28:16)

Paul prayed for a safe trip, and he arrived safely—after
getting arrested, shipwrecked and bitten by a poisonous
snake. God' way of answering our prayers are often far
from what we expected. When we pray, seeking God's
will, He will answer, but His ways and timing may be
different than we had hoped for.

"God, who has called you into fellowship with his Son
Jesus Christ, is faithful." (I Corinthians 1:9)

Be discerning in how you pray,
For God answers in His own way.

August 26

The Holy Spirit

*The Spirit of truth. The world cannot accept him,
because it neither sees him nor knows him. But you
know him, for he lives with you and will be in you.*
John 14:17 NIV

Many believers are unaware of the Holy Spirit's
activities but to those who hear Christ's words and
understand the Spirit's power, the Spirit gives a whole
new way to look at life. To have the Holy Spirit is to
have Jesus himself , for He is the Spirit of Christ.

The Holy Spirit is the very presence of God within every
believer, helping us to live as God desires and building
Christ's church on earth. By faith we can appropriate
the Spirit's power each day.

As we study the Bible we can trust Him to plant truth
into our minds, convince us of God's will and remind us
when we stray from it.

The end result of the Spirit's work in our life is a deep
and lasting peace. This peace is confident assurance
in any circumstance. The Spirit recognizes our
emotional and mental state and knows where we are
in our Christian growth. He will bring to our mind the
Scripture that will encourage, challenge or convict as
needed.

August 27

What is Life?

Why, you do not even know what will happen tomorrow.
What is your life? You are a mist that appears for a
little while and vanishes. James 4:14 NIV

The definition of life is on every tombstone: A dash between birth and death. Born –Died.

Our heavenly Father has a unique plan for every person's life, but He means for all of us to share one goal: to be conformed to the image of Christ. (To become more like Christ) Romans 8:28-29.

The process of perfecting our moral, spiritual and physical selves begins here on earth and is finished in Heaven. Much of the work God does in our earthly life centers on our character. He shows us how to be as loving, kind and peaceful as Jesus. He doesn't require us to do this on our own.

The Holy Spirit indwells the believer and lives the life of Christ through him or her. Christians have the responsibility to be submissive to Him.

The Sovereign Lord is behind what happens to us— either directly (causes) or indirectly (allows)—whether good or bad.

The more time I spend with Christ, through prayer and Bible Study, the more I become like Him.

August 28

Knowing God

This is what the Lord says:

Let not the wise man boast of his wisdom or the strong man boast of his strength or the rich man boast of his riches, but let him who boasts boast about this. That he understands and knows me, that I am the Lord, who exercises kindness, justice and righteousness on earth, for in these I delight, declares the Lord.

Jeremiah 9:23-24

People tend to admire four qualities in others: human wisdom, power (strength), kindness and riches. But God puts a higher priority on knowing Him personally and living a life that reflects His justice and righteousness.

This is a lifelong pursuit into eternity as we grow in our walk with the Lord.

"Now this is eternal life: that they may know you the only true God, and Jesus Christ whom you have sent." (John 17:3) This was the prayer of Jesus before He returned to the Father in heaven. This would glorify the Father and the Son. We were created for this purpose.

In Christ, the believer has been recreated and indwelt by His spirit to enable us to fulfill God's purpose.

August 29

Our Goal

I consider everything a loss compared to the surpassing greatness s of knowing Christ Jesus my Lord.
Philippians 3:8

A person's relationship with God, through Christ, is more important than anything in this world. To know Christ should be our ultimate goal.

What is my priority in life? Do I place anything above my relationship with Christ? Do I need to reorder my priorities?

It is a great tragedy that many people go through life without ever becoming acquainted with their Creator. To overlook that relationship is to miss the purpose of their existence and the greatest privilege available to mankind—Knowing God.

Though believers accept Christ, as their Savior, serve Him and anticipate being with Him in Heaven, many have no hunger to know Him better now. Salvation is God's free gift, but intimacy with Him is a costly process.

Our fellowship with the Lord should become more exciting and satisfying as the years go by.

Knowing God takes faith, focus and follow-through. Faith in who God is—focus on what He does—follow-through in obedience to His Word.

August 30

Christ

The Word became flesh and made his dwelling among us. We have seen his glory, the glory of the one and only, who came from the Father, full of grace and truth.
John 1:14 NIV

The Word was God's Beloved Son, Jesus, who was born in human flesh and dwelt on earth with mankind. John said, "We saw Him and walked with Him. We saw His glory. He was full of grace and truth."

Jesus was all that the Father is.

In His humanity He became:

1) The perfect teacher—we see how God thinks and how we should think. (Philippians 2:5-11)
2) The perfect example—a model of what we are to become. He shows us how to live and gives us the power to live that way. (I Peter 2:21)
3) The perfect sacrifice—Jesus came as the sacrifice for all sins, and His death satisfied God's requirement for the removal of sin. (Colossians 1:15-23)

Christ is the perfect expression of God in human form. We error when we try to minimize His humanity or His divinity. Jesus is both God and man.

The one who had authority over all creation walked this earth in complete submission to the Father's will. (John 5:19, 30)

August 31

Prayer

Ask and it will be given you; seek and you will find;
knock and the door will be opened to you.
Matthew 7:7.

God is more willing to answer our prayers than we are willing to pray. Too often we refuse to acknowledge our dependence upon God until we have failed in our own efforts.

When our children ask for something they need we don't ignore them or give them something that will harm them. We have a desire to provide for their needs. Ask God. Seek His will. Pursue His answer. Jesus said, "How much more will your Father in heaven give good gifts to those who ask." (v. 11)

James 4: 2-1—You do not have, because you do not ask God. When you ask, you do not receive, because you ask for the wrong things or the wrong reasons (motive).

Our heavenly Father knows our needs before we ask. Jesus said, "Seek first His kingdom and His righteousness, and all f these things will be given to you as well. (Matthews 6:33)

September

September 1

Prayer

For we do not have a high priest who is unable to sympathize with our weaknesses, but we have one who has been tempted in every way, just as we are—yet was without sin.

Hebrews 4:15 NIV

Jesus has more authority than the Jewish high priest because He is both man and God. As the Son of Man He intercedes for us before the Father. As the Son of God He assures us of God's forgiveness.

The Jewish priest could go before God only once a year on behalf of the people. Christ is always at the right hand of God to hear our prayers and to intercede for us. He can sympathize with our weaknesses because He went through the same temptations while on earth.

In each weakness Jesus turned to the Father. The Word of God was His defense in temptation, prayer was His source of strength in ministry and submission to the Father's will was the pathway to victory over sin and death.

The Word of God is my protection, prayer is my strength and submission to the Father is my way to victory over sin.

September 2

God's Will

*Who, then, is the man who fears the Lord? He will
instruct him in the way chosen for him.*
Psalm 25:12 NIV

To fear the Lord is to recognize God for who He is: holy, almighty, righteous, pure, all-knowing, all-powerful and all-wise. He is present everywhere.

When we see God as He is, we can get a clearer picture of ourselves: sinful, weak, helpless, needy. When we see who God is, and who we are, then we can bow before Him in humble reverence and respect.

When we are willing to seek God, learn from His Word and obey His commands, then we will receive His guidance.

"The Lord confides in those who fear Him; he makes his covenant known to them." (v. 14)

> Lord, teach me what I need to know.
> Show me where I need to go.
> I want to know your will and way,
> And follow You each passing day.

September 3

Christ's Return

While people are saying "Peace and safety," destruction will come on them suddenly, as labor pains on a pregnant woman, and they will not escape.
I Thessalonians 5:3 NIV

"The day of the Lord" is a future time when God will intervene directly in world affairs. Christ will judge sin and set up His eternal kingdom. The time will include both punishment and blessing.

1) Christ will return visibly with a loud command.

2) There will be an unmistakable cry from an angel.

3) There will be a trumpet sound as never heard before.

4) Believers in Christ who are dead will rise from their graves.

5) Believes who are alive will be caught up in the clouds to meet Christ.

We don't know the time of His coming but we know God is faithful to His promises and he has warned us to be ready for His coming.

September 4

Salvation

*The god of this age has blinded the minds of
unbelievers, so that they cannot see the light of the gospel
of the gory of Christ, who is the image of God.*
II Corinthians 4:4 NIV

The Gospel is open to everyone except to those who refuse to believe. Satan is the "god of this age." He is the "deceiver" and he uses money, power and pleasure to blind people to the light of Christ's Gospel.

Jesus Christ, God's Son, came to earth and was crucified, as our substitute, to satisfy God's judgment for sin. He has given us, who accept Him as our substitute, eternal life—in His presence for eternity.

In dying for us, Christ secured our salvation by paying the debt for all our past, present and future sins.

The tragedy is that many reject the Gospel—the death, burial and resurrection of Christ.

September 5

Abiding in Christ

I am the vine; you are the branches. If a man remains in me and I in him, he will bear much fruit; apart from me you can do nothing.
John 15:5 NIV

You did not choose me, but I chose you and appointed you to go and bear fruit—fruit that will last. Then the Father will give you whatever you ask in my name. John 15:16 NIV

Christ the True Vine, chose me as one of His branches, through whom He would produce fruit that would continue to demonstrate His likeness and nature. The result would be prevailing prayer, in His name, to bring the will of the Father in heaven, down to earth.

Fruit is not limited to soul-winning but involved the fruit of the Spirit mentioned in (Galatians 5:22-24), and answered prayer mentioned in (verse 16 above).

Remaining in Christ means staying connected with Christ in fellowship through prayer, Bible study and obedience.

September 6

Waiting on the Lord

*I wait for the lord, my soul waits, and in his word I put
my hope. Psalm 130:5*

*We wait in hope for the lord; He is our help and our
shield. Psalm 33:20*

All God's words are true. Unlike people, God does
not lie, forget or change His mind. We can trust the
Bible because it is the word of a holy, trustworthy and
unchangeable God.

The first step in waiting for the Lord is submission to
His will in how and when He will act. Right timing is
most important in our walk with the Lord. God is the
Creator and Ruler of time and He can never be late.

Waiting on the Lord requires faith. To wait for the
Lord means to pause for further instruction while
remaining in the present circumstance—a choice to be
actively still and quiet in our hearts while listening and
watching for His intervention.

September 7

Godliness

For physical training is of some value, but godliness has value for all things, holding promise for both the present life and the life to come.
I Timothy 4:8

But godliness with contentment is great gain.
I Timothy 6:6

In our society, much emphasis is placed on physical fitness, but spiritual health (godliness) is even more important. Our physical health is subject to disease and injury, but faith can sustain us through these difficulties. To train ourselves to be godly, we must nurture our faith by using our God-given abilities through which we grow in grace and knowledge of God.

Because thinking shapes beliefs, and beliefs determine our lifestyle, a biblical mindset is important in our Christian walk. Each day we choose to let either the world or God's Word shape our thoughts. We are quick to say we believe the Bible but sometimes our actions do not match our words.

A solid foundation of faith and wisdom starts with going to the Scriptures for direction.

September 8

Truth

We must pay more careful attention, therefore, to what we have heard, so that we do not drift away.
Hebrews 2:1

In Chapter 1, the writer of Hebrews is proclaiming the superiority of Christ. Christ is greater than angels, Moses and the Old Testament priesthood. Angels are servants, ministering spirits sent to serve those who will inherit salvation. (Hebrews 1:14) Christ is God's Son, our Savior. (Hebrews 1:5)

Therefore, we must pay attention to what God's word says so we will not drift away from the truth and fall into false teaching.

There is no end to the false teaching that is being spread throughout the world today. Religions and cults are multiplying daily as Satan continues his deception. The Believer's weapon of defense is God's Truth—His Written Word (the Bible) and His Living Word, The Lord Jesus Christ.

Jesus answered, "I am the way and the truth and the life. No one comes to the Father except through me."

Christ is our only security in a changing world. Whatever may happen in this world, Christ remains forever the same.

September 9

The Flesh and the Spirit

*I know that nothing good lives in me, that is, in my
sinful nature. For I have the desire to do what is good,
but I cannot carry it out. Romans 7:18*

*For the sinful nature desires what is contrary to the
Spirit and the Spirit what is contrary to the sinful
nature. They are in conflict with each other, so that they
do not do what you want. Galatians 5:17*

Paul had learned some lessons as he tried to deal with
his old sinful nature. (1) Knowledge is not the answer.
(2) Self determination doesn't work. (3) Becoming
a Christian does not keep sin and temptation from a
person's life.

Being born again takes a moment of faith but becoming
like Christ is a life-long process. We must never
underestimate the power of sin or attempt to fight it in
our own strength. Only through the power of Christ,
that is available to us, can we claim victory over sin and
temptation.

September 10

Our Shepherd

He tends his flock like a shepherd; he gathers his lambs in his arms and carries them close to his heart; he gently leads those who have young. Isaiah 40:11

There are many references in scripture to God as a Shepherd. The most familiar one is found in the Psalms. Psalm 23 is a favorite of many Christians as well as some unbelievers. It is a favorite for funerals because of its comforting message in the expression of God's love.

David, a shepherd himself, is the author of many of the Psalms. In Acts 13:22, we read that God spoke of David as being "a man after My own heart." His desire was for God. (Psalm 42:1-2) He thought of God as his Shepherd who watched over him night and day. He spent hours in fellowship with God, meditating upon the wonders of His person and power. He shares much of this through the Psalms.

Sometimes we miss a special message that God wants to share with us because we are not willing to spend time meditating on His word. One of these is found in Psalms 22, 23 and 24. These chapters should be studied as a group. They describe the life and ministry of Jesus as our Shepherd.

In the New Testament, Jesus is referred to as:

> The Good Shepherd—Past—John 10:11, 13
> The Great Shepherd—Present—Hebrews 13:20
> The Chief Shepherd—Future—I Peter 5:4

September 11

The Good Shepherd

*I am the good shepherd. The good shepherd lays down
his life for the sheep. John 10:11*

Psalm 22—Past

This Psalm is a prayer by David at a time of great distress in his life. A prayer that leads us from great suffering to great joy, It is also a prophecy concerning the deep agony Christ would endure on the cross, years later, when He took our place in death to pay the penalty for sin.

Despite David's feeling that he had been rejected by his friends, and God, he believed that God would lead him out of despair. He looked forward to the future when God would rule over the entire earth. David was not aware of the prophecy he had proclaimed concerning the Good Shepherd who would come to earth and die for the sin of all mankind. He knew God was on His Throne and one day the Messiah would reign over all. (verses 27, 28)

Today as we read David's prayer, and prophecy, we know that it happened as it was foretold and Jesus fulfilled His ministry as the Good Shepherd. His last words were "It is finished." (John 17:30) The debt was paid in full. God's plan of salvation was complete. "The good Shepherd laid down his life for the sheep."

Psalm 22 Fulfillment of Prophecy
Matthew 27
John 19-22:1, 2 - Matthew 27:46

Jesus was not questioning God; He was quoting the first line of Psalm 22. His prayer in the Garden was about his separation from the Father.

v. 7-8—Matthew 27: 39, 44, 43
v. 14-18—John 19:28, 34, 24
v. 27-28—Romans 14:11

September 12

The Great Shepherd

May the God of peace, who through the blood of the eternal covenant brought back from the dead our Lord Jesus, that great Shepherd of the sheep, equip you with everything good for doing his will, and may he work in us what his pleasing to him through Jesus Christ, to whom be glory for ever and ever. Amen.

Psalm 23 Present   *Hebrews 13:20-21*

In Psalm 23, David describes the ministry of Jesus, the Great Shepherd, after His resurrection. How He would work in the life of the believer, through His Holy Spirit, to provide for our needs in this life and in eternity. (II Peter 1:3-4) (Philippians 4:19) He sees God as a caring Shepherd and a dependable guide. He is our hope and security.

In verses 1-3, David talks <u>about</u> His Shepherd, His presence and provisions. In verses 4-5, David talks <u>to</u> his Shepherd about His power and His protection. Finally, David expresses his joy in the fact that the Great Shepherd is his personal Shepherd. (v. 6)

September 13

The Chief Shepherd

And when the Chief Shepherd appears, you will receive the crown of glory that will never fade away.
I Peter 5:4

Psalm 24   Future

David has talked about the Good Shepherd, who gave His life for His sheep and the Great Shepherd who protects and provides for His sheep. Now he shares about the Chief Shepherd, who will reign as Lord of Lords and King of Kings over His sheep. He declares God to be sovereign over all. The Creator of all is the Lord Almighty, the King of Glory.

As Chief Shepherd, Christ will gather His sheep to be with Him in eternity. He will reward His sheep with a "crown of glory" that will never fade away.

"Father, I want those you have given me to be with me where I am, and to see my glory, the glory you have given me because you loved me before the creation of the world." (John 17:24)

The truly powerful nation is not the one with a strong military, but rather the one who relies on God's caring strength—the Good, Great and Chief Shepherd.

September 14

Prayer With A Purpose

*I urge, then, first of all, that requests, prayers,
intercession, and thanksgiving be made for everyone—
for kings and all those in authority, that we may live
peaceful and quiet lives in all godliness and holiness.
This is good, and pleases God our Savior, who wants all
men to be saved and come to a knowledge of the truth.*

I Timothy 2:1-4

Praying for people is the right thing to do. The greatest
gift we can give anyone is to pray for that person. We
spend hours complaining about people and situations,
knowing that we are helpless to changing either.

Only God can do the impossible or make a way where
there is no way and He has told us to pray.

Some guidelines on how to intercede for others:

> Pray for spiritual enlightenment.
> Pray for a repentant spirit.
> Pray for their freedom from captivity.
> Claim them for Christ. (Expect spiritual warfare)
> Pray believing. (Matthew 21:22)
> Be alert to God's working.
> Pray for spiritual growth.
> Thank God for His faithfulness to His promises.

September 15

The Church

*As you come to him, the living Stone—you also, like
living stones, are being built into a spiritual house to be
a holy priesthood, offering spiritual sacrifices acceptable
to God through Jesus Christ.*
I Peter 2:4-5 NIV

Peter draws on some Old Testament scriptures to
portray the Church.

"The stone the builders rejected has become the
capstone." (Psalm 118:22)

"See, I lay a stone in Zion, a chosen and precious
cornerstone, and the one who trusts in him will never
be put to shame." (Isaiah 28:16)

Peter describes the Church as a living spiritual house
with Christ as the foundation (cornerstone), and each
believer as a stone.

Paul portrays the Church as a body, with Christ as the
head and each believer as a member of the body.

Both pictures emphasize community. Dependence
upon one another. What stone really counts in building the Church? Peter's answer: Christ Himself. As
the "cornerstone," He is the firm foundation. As the
"capstone," He is the center, holding it together—the
most important part.

"To those who believe He is precious. But to those who do not believe, He is a stumbling block, a rock that makes them fall." (I Peter 2:8)

Some will stumble over Christ because they reject Him. People who refuse to believe in Christ have made the greatest mistake of their lives. They have stumbled over the one person who could save them and give meaning to their lives.

September 16

Trusting Our Conscience

Now this is our boast: our conscience testifies that we have conducted ourselves in the world, and especially in our relations with you, in the holiness and sincerity that are from God. We have done so not according to worldly wisdom but according to God's grace.
II Corinthians 1:12 NIV

A common saying we often hears is, "Let your conscience be your guide." Can we depend on our conscience in every circumstance? Not unless we have trained our minds, according to God's principles and standards, to guide our behavior.

The conscience looks at thoughts and actions to determine if they are in line with our moral belief. If not, our internal alarm system, the Holy Spirit, alerts us. (John 16:13) "When the spirit of truth comes, he will guide you in all truth. (To know right from wrong).

When our habits reflect godly values, our conscience will become more sensitive to what is right and wrong. This will happen as we apply God's Word to our daily living. (Romans 12:2)

September 17

Praying for Others

*Since the day we heard about you, we have not stopped
praying for you and asking God to fill you with the
knowledge of his will through all spiritual wisdom and
understanding. And we pray this in order that you may
live a life worthy of the Lord and may please him in
every way.*

Colossians 1:9-10a

We often pray for family and friends in a general way,
asking God to bless, protect and provide for them. God
will honor these prayers but there is a more powerful
way to pray—using Gods Word, His promises, His
desires makes our prayers more specific and personal.
Paul's prayers are good examples for us as we pray for
others when we do not know their special need.

We can request that they:

Gain spiritual wisdom and understanding of God's will.

Please and honor God and bear good fruit.

Grow in the knowledge of God.

Be filled with God's strength and patience.

Stay full of Christ's joy and give thanks always.

All believers have these same basic needs. One of the
greatest gifts we can give is to lift a person in prayer.

September 18

The Old Paths

Stand at the crossroads and look; ask for the ancient paths, ask where the good way is, and walk in it, and you will find rest for your souls. But you said, We will not walk in it. I appointed watchmen over you and said, Listen to the sound of the trumpet! But you said, We will not listen.

Jeremiah 6:16-17

The right path for living is ancient and has been marked out by god. But the people refused to take God's path, going their own way instead.

We face the same decision today—going God's old way, the true way, or following a new path of our own choosing. Don't be misled. The only way to find peace and "rest for your soul" is to walk on God's path.

We need to evaluate life daily and get back to the basics recorded in God's Word.

It's not about me, myself and I,
It's about He who was willing to die.

September 19

God's Power

*Do you not know? Have you not heard? The Lord is the
everlasting God, the creator of the ends of the earth. He
will not grow tired or weary, and his understanding
no one can fathom. He gives strength to the weary and
increases the power of the weak.*
Isaiah 40:28-29

Isaiah describes God's power to create, His provision to
sustain and His presence to help. There is no one who
can be compared to Him. Even the strongest people
get tired at times but God's power and strength never
diminish and His strength is our source of strength.
He is never too tired to help or too busy to listen.

"God is our refuge and strength, an ever present help
in trouble." Psalm 46:1

Don't try to be good in your own strength. God didn't
make these human bodies, mind and spirit to live on
our own but to "live in Christ."

September 20

Patience

Wait for the Lord; be strong and take heart and wait on the Lord.

Psalm 27:14

On an old Grandfather clock in Chester Cathedral, England, is the inscription:

> "When as a child I laughed and wept,
> Time crept.
> When as a youth, I dreamed and talked,
> Time walked.
> When I became a man,
> Time ran.
> And later as I older grew,
> Time flew.
> Soon I shall find, while traveling on,
> Time gone."

Patience is not a natural attribute. It is mentioned as a "fruit of the Spirit" in Galatians 5:22. We sometimes hear the comment, "Lord, give me patience." Maybe we need to consider why we are in a trying situation. The Lord may be trying to teach us patience, but we're not listening.

September 21

Lord of All

So then, just as you received Christ Jesus as Lord,
continue to live in him.
Colossians 2:6

When Christ is Lord in my life He is Lord of all. If He is not Lord of all, He is not Lord at all. If I refuse to allow Christ to be Lord of all that I am and Lord of all that I have, He is not my Lord.

I received Christ through faith and obedience and I am to continue living in Him through faith and obedience.

I cannot do this on my own but when I accepted Christ into my life His Spirit came into my heart as my Helper and Teacher. He enables me to be and do what God has planned for my life. He works for me, in me and through me for God's glory.

Christ won the victory on Calvary.
He paid the penalty of sin for me.
His grace, through faith has set me free,
To be the person I was created to be.

September 22

Knowing God

*The Lord is a refuge for the oppressed, a stronghold in times
of trouble. Those who know your name will trust in you, for
you, Lord, have never forsaken those who seek you.*
Psalm 9:-10 NIV

We all have times of doubt when we feel that God has
forgotten us. We want to trust Him more but aren't
really sure how to do so. The key lies in knowing the
Lord and claiming His promises for He is faithful to
His Word.

God is sovereign. (Psalm 103:19) He is in control of all.

God is infinitely wise. (Romans 11:33-36) He knows
the inside and outside of every situation and event
(past, present and future).

His love is perfect. (Exodus 34:6) He chooses what is
best for us, even if it's not easy.

We come to know Him better as we spend time with
Him in His Word and prayer.

September 23

The Peace of God

*I have told you these things, so that in me you may
have peace. In this world you will have trouble but take
heart! I have overcome the world.*
John 16:33 NIV

As I read the paper and watch T.V. I tell myself that I
am not for this world anymore. I feel out of place. I'm
reminded of the song "This world is not my home, I'm
just passing through." I can rejoice, at these times,
because the peace of God is mine, in Christ. Though
the world is in turmoil and I am experiencing troubles,
I know that Christ has overcome the world and His
Spirit indwells me to enable me to claim His victory as
mine.

"In all these things we are more than conquerors
through Him who loved us." (Romans 8:37)

Thank you, Lord, for your faithfulness to your promises.

September 24

Prayer

And I will do whatever you ask in my name, so that the
Son may bring glory to the Father. You may ask me for
anything in my name, and I will do it.
John 14:13-14

What does it mean to ask for something "in Jesus' name?" Jesus is talking about a new relationship between the believer and God. When Jesus came as Savior His ministry involved three positions—Prophet, Priest and King. As Prophet He is the Living Word; as Priest He is our Mediator; as King He is our Lord.

After Jesus' resurrection all believers are priests in Him, and can talk with God personally and directly in Jesus' Name, that is, according to His character and will. Through the blood of Jesus we have been made acceptable to the Father.

If we are sincerely following God and seeking to do His will then our request will be in line with what He wants and He will grant our request. (John 15:16; 16:23)

September 25

Eternal Life

*I tell you the truth, whoever hears my word and believes
him who sent me has eternal life and will not be
condemned; he has crossed over from death to life"*

John 5:24

Eternal life—living forever with God—begins when we
accept Jesus Christ as Savior. New life begins in you
at that moment. It is a completed transaction. We will
still face physical death but when Christ returns our
body will be resurrected to live forever. (I Thessalonians
5:14-18)

God is the source and Creator of life. There is no life
apart from God, here or hereafter. Physical death is
not the end as some unbelievers think. Those who have
rejected Christ will be resurrected also to be judged and
condemned to eternity apart from God.

September 26

Stress

God is our refuge and strength, an ever present help in trouble.
Psalm 46:1

We hear a lot of talk about "stress" in our world today. We experience pressure from many different sources— wars, economic crisis, insecurity - even simple things like traffic and daily responsibilities can become stressful. Stress becomes "distress" when it creates emotional and mental anxiety.

Jesus assured us that, though we would face difficulty, we could rest in Him. (John 16:33) Seeking the truth of God's Word will encourage us during these times. This helps us to understand how He thinks. (Romans 15:4) Watching how God works in other people's lives will help us to know His ways.

God loves us and He wants us to trust Him, lean on Him and let Him carry our burdens. We can read the Bible, pray, meditate on His Word and listen quietly for His Spirit to speak to our hearts.

September 27

Our Hope

Now we know that if the earthly tent (our body) we live in is destroyed, we have a building from God, an eternal house in heaven, not built by human hands. Meanwhile we groan, longing to be clothed with our heavenly dwelling.

II Corinthians 5:1-2

As we age this earthly tent (our body) deteriorates and ceases to function as it did in our younger years. Physically, we are limited in many ways—mentally, we are less alert. We often become confused and frustrated. Paul says, "We groan," longing for heaven and become burdened because of our condition.

This is the season in our life when we really learn to live by faith rather than by sight. (v. 7) The things we see are temporal but God has something much better prepared for us—a body that will never grow old. God has not revealed, in detail, what our body will be like but we know our soul and spirit will be clothed in a perfect body, suited for eternity. We will not be found naked (without a body).

September 28

Power Within

*But you will receive power when the Holy Spirit comes
on you, and you will be my witnesses in Jerusalem and
in Judea and Samaria and to the ends of the earth.*

Acts 1:8

If you believe in Jesus Christ, you can experience the
power of the Holy Spirit in your life. God's plan for
making Himself known to the world is through those
who believe Him, and His Son, whom He has sent
into the world. God's Spirit works in every believer
to produce godly character and conduct that bears
witness of God's work in our lives.

The "fruit of the Spirit," His work in our lives, is the
most powerful message we can give to the world. It
is the way we respond when under pressure, problems
and temptations.

The most powerful witness where you work, where you
live and where you relax is "you."

September 29

Satanic Attacks

Finally be strong in the Lord and in his mighty power.
Put on the full armor of God so that you can take your
stand against the devil's schemes.
Ephesians 6:10-11

A satanic attack is an assault upon an individual, to cause spiritual, physical, material or emotional harm.

The devil is real. Scripture tells us that he leads an army of fallen angels and thinks he can overcome God. We cannot stand against him in our own power but Christ in the believer is greater than Satan. (I John 4:4)

The battle begins in our mind. We must be very selective in our thinking by allowing the Holy Spirit to guide our thoughts as we spend time in God's Word. Satan tempts when we are hungry, angry, lonely or tired.

As Christians, we can practice the presence of Christ when we read the Word, pray and fellowship with other believers. These are weapons we can use against Satan in spiritual warfare.

September 30

God's Direction

*Show me your ways, O Lord, teach me your paths; guide
me in your truth and teach me, for you are God my
Savior, and my hope is in you all day long. Psalm 25:4-5*

How do we receive God's guidance?

The first step is to want to be guided and to realize that
God's primary guidance system is His Word, the Bible.
Psalm 119 tells of the endless knowledge found in God's
Word. By reading it and learning from it we will gain the
wisdom to know God's direction for our lives. When we
are willing to seek God, learn from His Word and obey
His commands, then we will receive specific guidance.

We are bombarded today with appeals to go in various
directions. Television advertising alone places hundreds
of options before us and appeals made by political parties,
cults, false religious and other groups. Numerous
organizations, including Christian groups, seek to
motivate us to support a cause. And then, the decisions
concerning our jobs, our family, our money and we
become desperate for someone to show us the right way.

"Who, then, is the man that fears the Lord? He will
instruct him in the way chosen for him." (Psalm 25:12)
To fear the Lord is to recognize God for who He is; Holy,
Almighty, Righteous, pure, all-knowing, all-powerful and
all-wise. When we see God as He is, we can see ourselves
as we are—totally dependent on Him.

On life's road, crucial decisions are like intersections that call for a choice of directions. Although the Lord is ready and willing to offer clear direction, He doesn't always give it quickly. If impatience tempts you to run ahead of God's timing, you risk missing His blessings.

October

October 1

The Model Prayer

*Our Father in heaven, hallowed be your name, your
kingdom come, your will be done on earth as it is in
heaven. Give us today our daily bread. Forgive us our
debts, as we also have forgiven our debtors. And lead us
not into temptation, but deliver us from the evil one.*

Matthew 6:9-13

We should praise God, pray for His work in the world,
pray for our daily needs and pray for help in our daily
struggles.

The phrase "Our Father in Heaven" reminds us that
God is holy and majestic and also loving and personal.
"Your kingdom come" is a reference to God's spiritual
reign that was announced in the covenant with Abraham.
(Matthew 8:11; Luke 13:28) It is present in Christ's reign
in believers' hearts (Luke 17:21) and will be complete
when all evil is destroyed and God establishes the New
Heaven and New Earth. (Revelations 21:1) "Your will
be done" is praying that God's perfect purpose will be
accomplished in this world as well as in the next. "Give
us today our daily bread" is acknowledging that God is
our provider and sustainer.

God doesn't lead us into temptations but sometimes
He allows us to be tested by them. We need God's
wisdom to recognize the subtle ways of the "evil one"
and His strength to overcome our daily struggles. (I
Corinthians 10:13)

October 2

Stress

*You will keep in perfect peace him whose mind is
steadfast, because he trusts in you. Trust in the Lord
forever, for the Lord, the Lord is the Rock eternal.*
Isaiah 26:3-4 NIV

Stress is a major problem in our world today, and its
source is self. Self-desire, self-control, self-satisfaction
and so on. Self can never satisfy self. Possessions,
power, pleasure seek more of the same.

God is the source of our being and we are created to
be dependent on Him. As we recognize that and turn
to Him, only then can we experience the peace that
passes understanding that God has promised.

How to begin:

Get rid of stuff you don't need—let go.

Get serious with God—recognize dependence on Him.

Focus on what really matters—people, not things.

Return to healthy routine—eat, work, rest, sleep.

"In quietness and confidence you will find peace."
(Quietness before God—confidence in God)

October 3

Reconciliation

We are therefore, Christ's ambassadors, as though God were making his appeal through us. We implore you on Christ's behalf: Be reconciled to God.

II Corinthians 5:20 NIV

When we see the word "therefore" in the Bible we need to check what it is there for. Here we find the answer in verse 19. God has committed to believers the message of reconciliation, through Christ. We are representatives of Christ to share this message with the world.

The message is:

How God has reconciled sinful man unto Himself through the death of Christ as our substitute. When we trust in Christ, we make an exchange—our sin for His righteousness. Our sin was poured into Christ at His crucifixion. His righteousness was poured into us at our conversion. (v. 21)

Christians are new on the inside—not reformed, rehabilitated, or re-educated—we are recreated, new creations (v. 17) in Christ Jesus.

October 4

Blessing Others

For surely, O Lord, you bless the righteous; you surround them with your favor as with a shield.
Psalm 5:12 NIV

Every day we enjoy the blessings of God, even when we are not aware we are being blessed. God's Word shares many ways through which these blessings come into our lives. He blesses us so we can bless others.

Often when I sneeze someone will say "Bless you." What is really involved in that common expression? What does it mean? Actually, it is a request for divine favor. Sometimes we express it to strangers. Is it just a cliché or a sincere desire from the heart?

How can we bless others?

We can bless people by praying for them.

We can ask God's favor on events and situations.

We can bless God by expressing our praise and thanksgiving for His character and for what He has done. We can also bless God through our obedience and desire to please Him.

October 5

The Rock of Ages

Therefore, everyone who hears these words of mine and puts them into practice is like a wise man who built his house on the rock. The rain came down, the stream rose, and the winds blew and beat against that house; yet it did not fall, because it had its foundation on the rock.

Matthew 7:24-25

Building "on the rock" means hearing and responding in a positive way. We know it is important to build on a solid foundation if we want a sense of security. Jesus used this natural principle to teach a spiritual truth.

When we build our life on Christ, the "Rock," we're on a solid foundation. When trials, temptations and anxiety threaten to overwhelm us we can stand secure on our faith in Christ.

A house of faith is constructed brick by brick as we pray, study God's Word and obey it in our daily life.

October 6

Consistency

*Now when Daniel learned that the decree had been
published, he went home to his upstairs room where the
windows opened toward Jerusalem. Three times a day
he got down on his knees and prayed, giving thanks to
his God, just as he had done before.*
Daniel 6:10

Daniel was over eighty years old, still in Babylonian
captivity. King Darius had signed a decree that anyone
found praying to any god or man, other than the King,
would be thrown into the lions' den.

Daniel had a disciplined prayer life. We find our
prayers are usually interrupted, not by threats, but by
the pressure of our schedules. We should never allow
our daily cares to take priority over our prayer time for
prayer is our lifeline to God.

Only God can provide for our needs and often in ways
we could never imagine.

God can even shut the lions' mouths!

October 7

Growth

*Like newborn babies, crave pure spiritual milk, so that
you may grow up in your salvation, now that you have
tasted that the Lord is good.*
I Peter 2:2-3 NIV

When we are "born again," we become spiritual newborn babies. The need for milk is natural for a baby
and it will lead to growth. The same is true for a new
babe in Christ. Natural milk is necessary for physical
growth. Spiritual milk (the Word) is necessary for spiritual growth.

Once we see our need for God's Word and begin to
find nourishment in Christ, the Living Water and the
Living Bread, our spiritual appetite will increase and
we will grow and mature.

Just as we need daily physical food we also need daily
spiritual food. We need to read the Word, meditate
on the Word, hide the Word in our heart and pray for
understanding of God's truth.

October 8

Praise

I will praise you, O Lord, with my whole heart; I will tell of all your wonders.
Psalm 9:1

Praise is expressing to God our appreciation and understanding of His worth. It's saying "thank you" for each aspect of His divine nature. Our inward attitude becomes an outward expression. When we praise God we help ourselves by expanding our awareness of who He is. We consider His character, His attributes. He is worthy of the praise of all creation.

When Jesus entered Jerusalem on "Palm Sunday" the crowds were joyfully praising God and the Pharisees asked Jesus to rebuke them. "I tell you," he replied, "If they keep quiet, the stones will cry out." (Luke 19:40)

The book of Psalms is a book of praise through which the writers have shared the many ways that God has revealed Himself. The last chapter is a special declaration of Praise. Praise the Lord!

October 9

Prepare for Battle

Be strong in the Lord and in his mighty power. Put on the full armor of God so that you can take your stand against the devil's schemes.
Ephesians 6:10-11

Why do we Christians fail so often to resist temptation and sin? Paul tells us that our struggle is not against flesh and blood (people) but: against the rulers, against the authorities, against the powers of this dark world and against the spiritual forces of evil in the heavenly realms (demons; fallen angels) under Satan's control. (v. 12)

Some reasons why we live defeated lives:

1) We are unaware of the battle, which makes us prime targets for attack.

2) We are ignorant about the enemy; don't understand his tactics or goals.

3) We are untrained for warfare; the training manual is God's Word.

4) We allow Satan a foothold. The battleground is the mind; thoughts, feelings and desires.

We must fill our minds with God's Word and be sensitive to the Holy Spirit's warning.

October 10

Wisdom

*The fear of the Lord is the beginning of wisdom, and
knowledge of the Holy One is understanding.*
Proverbs 9:10

When we think of the word "fear" we associate it
with an emotional response to something bad. There
is another definition of fear that refers to respect or
reverence for someone. This is the word used in the
Bible when referring to God as the Holy and Righteous
One. We recognize Him as the sovereign ruler of
heaven and earth and as a result we become wise.

There is a difference between wisdom and knowledge.
Knowledge is information; it has to do with intellect.
Wisdom has to do with heart and attitude—viewing life
from God's perspective. A good definition—wisdom is
the ability to use the knowledge we have.

When we "fear" God we will have a desire to please
Him in what we do and say.

October 11

Worry

*Therefore I tell you, do not worry about your life, what
you will eat or drink; or about your body, what you will
wear. But seek first his kingdom and his righteousness,
and all these things will be given to you as well.*

Matthew 6:25, 33

This is one of God's amazing promises that we read but
never stop and consider what God is trying to tell us.
We are so focused on what the world thinks is important that we fail to see where our priorities should be.
We forget the source of our being—our Provider and
protector—why we are here and where we are going.

To "seek first his kingdom and his righteousness:"
means to turn to God first for help and think about His
desires for us. He knows what worry can do in our life—
physically, mentally, emotionally and spiritually—and
his desire is to protect us from those experiences by
supplying our needs. Trust Him!

October 12

Knowing God

I consider everything a loss compared to the surpassing greatness of knowing Christ Jesus my Lord.
Philippians 3:8

A person's relationship with God, through the Lord Jesus Christ, is the most important thing in this life. To know Christ should be our ultimate goal.

What is my priority in life?
Do I place anything above my relationship with Christ?
Do I need to reorder my priorities?

I need to grow in my knowledge of God by focusing on my relationship with Him through Christ. It is a great tragedy that many people go through life without becoming acquainted with their Creator. To overlook that relationship is to miss the purpose of their existence and the greatest privilege available to mankind—knowing God.

Though believers can accept Christ as their Savior, serve Him and anticipate going to Heaven, many have no hunger to know Him in a more intimate way while on earth.

Salvation is a free gift but true intimacy with God is a costly process. However, the rewards are invaluable and eternal.

October 13

All or Nothing

Why do you call me, 'Lord, Lord' and do not do what I say? Luke 6:46

When Christ is Lord of my life He is Lord of all. If he is not Lord of all He is not Lord at all. If I refuse to allow Christ to be Lord of all that I am and Lord of all that I have, He is not my Lord.

What does it mean for Christ to be Lord of my life?

1) Ask Christ to come into my heart and save me from my sin (the penalty of sin which is death—separation from God.)
2) Ask Christ to take control of my life and lead me in His will (conform me to His image—make me like Him.)
3) Have a desire, always, to know His ways and to be obedient to Him.
4) Fellowship with Him each day through prayer and Bible reading (I share with Him through prayer. He shares with me through His word, the Bible.)

I cannot do any of this by myself but when I take the first step—ask Christ to come into my heart –Christ's Spirit will dwell in my heart to teach me and help me to be what God wants me to be and to do what God wants me to do. The first step is a one-time experience for the Holy Spirit never leaves me after He indwells me. The other three steps—asking Christ to take control, desiring to know His ways and to be obedient are daily experiences through faith.

October 14

My Purpose

So whether you eat or drink or whatever you do, do it all
for the glory of God.
I Corinthians 10:31

Why do I read my Bible?

> To know God, His ways, His works and His will.
> Why? To be obedient and to share with others.
> Why? To glorify God.

Why do I pray?

> To know God more intimately through
> communion and fellowship. Why? To experience
> His working in a personal way, in and through
> me. Why? To glorify God.

Why do I give?

> To express my love and obedience to God. Why?
> So others can know Him, because he loved us
> and gave Himself for us. Why? To glorify God.

Why do I serve?

> To fulfill His purpose in my life and to build up
> the Body of Christ. Why? To express His love
> for me and others. Why? To Glorify God.

October 15

Eternal Life

*I write these things to you who believe in the name of
the Son of God so that you may know that you have
eternal life.*

I John 5:13

To have a clear understanding of eternal security you
must understand what is involved, what took place, in
salvation.

Adam's sinful nature is reproduced in every person
through physical birth. We were born alienated from
God because of that sinful nature. There is nothing
more we can do to change that. Only God, who created
man, can recreate man. He has chosen to do this
through His Son, the Lord Jesus Christ, who was
conceived of the Holy Spirit, without sin, and lived a
life without sin. He died as man's substitute, to pay
the penalty for the sin of all mankind.

Only through the death of Christ can we be reconciled
to God. When we accept Christ's death as our death
to sin and His resurrection as our resurrection to life,
then His righteousness becomes our righteousness.
Our sins past, present and future, have been paid for
and nothing can change that. I'm secure in Christ!

My definition of "Abundant Life"

"Experiencing and enjoying all that God has provided
for me, in Christ, and sharing it with others."

October 16

Forgiveness

*Be kind and compassionate to one another, forgiving
each other, just as in Christ God forgave you.*
Ephesians 4:32

Unforgiveness is one of the most destructive behaviors
possible. It can affect every part of our being; our
prayers, relationships, thoughts, attitudes and actions.

As we consider God's mercy and forgiveness toward
us, how can we withhold forgiveness toward others? It
shows a lack of "oneness" with Christ.

What is forgiveness? It is giving up resentment toward
someone, with no desire to retaliate. It involves the
attitude that declares, "Though you wronged me, I love
and forgive you. I wish you the best and I will help you
however I can."

Pray for the one who wrongs you and release your
resentment.

October 17

Prayer

The end of all things is near. Therefore be clear minded
and self-controlled so that you can pray.
I Peter 4:7

Getting ready to meet Christ involves continuing to grow in love for God and others. We are to be sensitive to God's leading, and to the needs of other people. Our possessions and worldly concerns will mean nothing in God's Kingdom (future) but we will spend eternity with God's people.

Time spent in prayer, growing in grace and knowledge of God, seeking His will and obeying His principles is an investment that will pay dividends for eternity.

One of the greatest things we can do for family and friends is to pray for them. God knows their needs but he works through the prayers of His people, not because He has to but because He has chosen to do so.

He may be waiting to hear from you before He does something special in someone's life. Take time to pray.

October 18

Praise

Let the word of Christ dwell in you richly in all wisdom,
teaching and admonishing one another in psalms and
hymns and spiritual songs, singing with grace in your
hearts to the Lord.
Colossians 3:16

The word "psalms" refers to actual Scripture set to music. "Hymns" are praise songs that express adoration directly to God. "Spiritual songs" include a variety of songs with a vital spiritual message.

One of the greatest expressions of fellowship among God's people is when they join together in songs of praise and worship to the Lord.

Psalm 147:1
  "Praise the Lord. How good it is to sing praises to our God, how pleasant and fitting to praise him!"

Psalm 33:1
  "Sing joyfully to the Lord, you righteous; it is fitting for the upright to praise him."

Because God is Creator, Lord and Savior, He is worthy to be praised. Because He is faithful and His word is true we can rejoice and sing, giving thanks and praise.

October 19

Assurance of Salvation

*How great is the love that the Father has lavished on us,
that we should be called children of God! And that is
what we are.*

I John 3:1

Whoever believes in God's Son has eternal life. (John 3:16) He is all you need. You don't have to wait, it begins the moment you believe. You don't need to work, it's already yours. You don't need to worry it is guaranteed. It is not based on feelings, but on facts.

Tests to remind us of our security:

The Word Test—God's Word—"Believe in the Lord Jesus and you will be saved." Acts 16:31

The Witness Test—The Spirit's testimony. "The Spirit Himself testifies with our spirit that we are God's children." Romans 8:16

The Walk Test—Christ's transforming grace. I am in Christ (takes care of the outside), Christ is in me (takes care of the inside). Galatians 2:20

I John 5:13
"I write these things unto you who believe in the name of the Son of God so that you may know that you have eternal life."

October 20

Unity in Christ

How great is the love that the Father has lavished on us,
that we should be called children of God! And that is
what we are.
I John 3:1

We are one Body—the fellowship of believers—the Church.

Indwelled by one Spirit—the Holy Spirit who activates the body.

With one Hope—that glorious future to which we are called.

Following one Lord—Christ to whom we all belong.

Exercising one Faith—Our singular commitment to Christ.

Experiencing one Baptism—The sign of entry into the Church.

Worshiping one God—Our Father who keeps us for eternity.

When believers have this unity of the Spirit (a spirit of unity), no differences should ever be allowed to dissolve that unity.

October 21

God at Work

For it is God who works in you to will and to act
according to his good purpose.
Philippians 2:13

God is at work everywhere. In the first verse of the Bible He is creating the heavens and the earth. In the last verse of Revelation He is calling people to be saved.

Our life may seem to be routine, but God is busy every day conforming us to the image of Christ. What appears to be slow to us is not slow to God. His timing is always perfect. (II Peter 3:8-9)

When I am truly depending on the Holy Spirit's power and wisdom I will:

1) Be aware that without God's active presence I will fail.
2) Seek to please God alone and not compromise.
3) Look expectantly for the Holy Spirit to be at work.
4) Spend more time thanking and praising God.
5) Exhibit joy, the fruit of the Spirit, instead of worry.

October 22

Obedience

Whoever has my commands and obeys them, he is the
one who loves me.
John 14:21

Love is more than lovely words; it is commitment and conduct. If I love Christ I can prove it by obeying what He says in His word. If I obey Jesus and align myself closely with God's purpose Satan can have no power over me. Conquering faith turns a deaf ear to discouragement.

Jesus saves the deepest revelations of Himself for those who love and obey Him.

When God tests us it is a good time to test Him by claiming His promises. Claim from Him just as much as your trials have made necessary. God tries our faith so that we may try His faithfulness.

God is the "Great I Am"—whatever I need, He is the answer.

October 23

Love

*And this commandment we have from Him, that the one
who loves God should love his brother also.*
I John 4:21 NASB

Love is not a feeling—love is a choice and action. God's
love is unconditional and His character is just. His love
is an unwavering commitment to what is in my best
interest. His love is perfect and the highest expression
of that love was demonstrated when Christ died on the
cross.

God is the source of our love and Jesus is our example
of what it means to love. The Holy Spirit gives us the
power to love. He lives in our heart to enable us to be
more like Christ.

Because God's nature is love He sacrificed the Son
He loved for the people He loved. His wrath against
sin was poured out upon His Son, who took man's
place in death (becoming sin) that man might become
righteous (have new life) in Him. What great love God
has bestowed upon us!

October 24

Discouragement

Have I not commanded you? Be strong and courageous.
Do not be terrified; do not be discouraged, for the Lord
your God will be with you wherever you go."
Joshua 1:9

Discouragement is one of Satan's most effective weapons. If he can destroy our courage he can play havoc in every area of our life. One of the marks of discouragement is a divided mind—not able to focus on what is at hand—a sense of confusion. It seems like a dark cloud hovers over our thoughts. There's no sense of God's presence; only a negative outlook.

Some spiritual causes:

1) Our prayers not answered. Lose hope. Stop praying.
2) Lack of communication with God can cause deeper discouragement.
3) Failure to understand God's Sovereignty and how He works.
4) Believing good works gains God's favor.
5) Doubt as to pleasing God.

God's love is based on His grace, not our deeds. If you want encouragement; claim God's promises.

October 25

The Bible

In the beginning was the Word, and the Word was with God, and the Word was God. He was with God in the beginning.
John 1:1-2

The word, "Word," used in this verse refers to Christ, the Living Word of God. The Bible is the Written Word of God, the history of the Living Word—"His Story."

The Bible is not a collection of fables or human ideas about God. It is God's very words given to people through people. God, who is Sovereign over all creation is also Sovereign over His Word. It is inspired, inerrant and infallible. Unless a person has a firm belief in the Sovereignty of God his concept of the truth of God's Word will be clouded.

Fulfilled prophecy is proof that the Word of God is never wrong. (Isaiah 48:3)

Our Creator wants us to know Him. He shares His thoughts with us and invites us to have an intimate relationship with Him. Every day we have the privilege of opening His Word and having a heart-to-heart conversation with our Loving God.

Don't ignore His invitation.

October 26

Man

Then God said, "Let us make man in our image,
according to our likeness----and God created man in His
own image, in the image of God He created him; male
and female he created them. Genesis 1:26-27 NAS

When Adam had lived one hundred and thirty years, he
became the father of a son in his likeness, according to
his image, and named him Seth. Genesis 5:3 NAS

When Adam had lived one hundred and thirty years, he
became the father of a son in his likeness, according to
his image, and named him Seth. Genesis 5:3 NAS

> Image—a representation
> Likeness—being like

Adam was to represent God in all creation. He ruled
over God's creation. When Adam disobeyed God, and
acted independently of Him, that relationship was
severed (God's Spirit moved out of Adam's spirit) and
ever thing changed. Sin, which Adam had not known,
entered the picture and continues today.

Adam became the father of a son in his likeness (a sinful
nature) which all mankind has inherited from the first
Adam. But God, in His grace has provided (through
Christ, the last Adam) for His spirit to reenter man'
spirit. God's Beloved Son, Jesus, became man and lived
a sinless life. He died to pay the penalty for man's sin.

When we accept Him as our substitute, in death, His
Spirit indwells us eternally. Our sinful nature is
transformed into a new nature.

October 27

Love

Yet I hold this against you; you have forsaken your first love.
Revelation 2:4

This was a warning from Christ to the Church at Ephesus. He had just commended them for all the good things they had done but they had a problem. They had been so busy working for God that they had no time to be with God.

This often happens in the life of a new Christian. It's easy to get so caught up in the joy and excitement of the new life in Christ (transformation from the natural to the spiritual) that our zeal overtakes our knowledge. When this happens our concept of God's love can be misguided.

God's love is based on His character (God is love. I John 4:8), not on what we do. Our misconception is that the more we do for God the more He will love us and the more He loves us the more we should do. It can become a cycle in our lifestyle.

Work for God must be motivated by love for God or it will not last. God desires an intimate relationship with us. That becomes a reality when we spend time with Him in prayer and His Word.

October 28

Salvation

For it is by grace you have been saved, through faith—
and this is not from yourselves, it is the gift of God.
Ephesians 2:8

When I read Ephesians 2:8 I am reminded that my salvation involves more than a gift from God - it involves the gift of God "Himself." This is the result of "agape love" and I am commanded to express this same love in death to self, for Christ, and in life of self for others.

This is what Jesus meant in John 15:13, "Greater love hath no man than this, that a man lay down his life for his friends. "We are not asked to die for our friends but to live for them. We are to allow God to bless others through us.

October 29

Giving

Now he who supplies seed to the sower and bread for food will also supply and increase your store of seed and will enlarge the harvest of your righteousness.

II Corinthians 9:10

God has promised to supply all I need to live and to give. We often express our desire to know God's will for our life—where we need to be and what we need to do—but how much time do we spend in seeking His will and desire concerning our finances?

The Lord graciously supplies us with incomes so we can provide for our needs and even our desires. "And God is able to make all grace abound to you, so that in all things at all times, having all that you need, you will abound in every good work." (II Corinthians 9:9)

God blesses us so we can be a blessing to others. This is His plan for His people and the principle concerning His plan is, "If you sow sparingly you will reap sparingly— if you sow generously you will reap generously." Be a joyful giver!

October 30

Rest

Find rest, O my soul, in God alone; my hope comes from Him. He alone is my rock and my salvation; he is my fortress, I will not be shaken.
Psalm 62:5-6

I can never grow in my relationship with God until I learn to wait upon Him. While I wait He is working—preparing hearts and arranging circumstances. I can rest assured He will respond in the best way at the right time. I must be sensitive to God's voice, read His Word and ask Him to speak to my heart—then I must trust Him. Faith is stretched and strengthened the most during hardship.

God's greatest joy comes from our genuine worship and trust. He reveals Himself to the degree that I open up my heart to Him, listen and then act upon what He shows me.

> Resting at the feet of Jesus,
> In the gory of His grace;
> Refreshing moments for my soul,
> In the radiance of His face.
> Learning of His boundless mercy,
> Overshadowed by His peace,
> Joyful in His calm assurance,
> That His love shall never cease.

October 31

Fear

So do not fear, for I am with you; do not be dismayed,
for I am your God. I will strengthen you and help you; I
will uphold you with my righteous right hand.
Isaiah 41:10

I need not fear for God is with me. He has established a relationship with me—I am his child. He gives me assurance of His strength, help and victory over sin and death.

One of Satan's oldest deceptions is the temptation to doubt what the Lord has said. Mistrusting God sets me up for the enemy. He will exaggerate details to make me believe things are worse than they actually are and I will begin to react to circumstances rather than obey God's Word in faith.

I need to look at my problems in light of God's power rather than looking at God in the shadow of my problems.

At a time in my life, when I was going through some physical problems, I claimed this promise, in faith, until I was restored. God is faithful and good.

November

In His Presence

Lord, who may dwell in your sanctuary? Who may live on your holy hill? He whose walk is blameless and who does what is righteous.

Psalm 15:1-2

The Psalmist is asking, "Who can enjoy the presence of God?" Being in the presence of God doesn't necessarily mean that we enjoy or that we are always aware of His presence. He is always present with the believer, in the person of the Holy Spirit, but if there is unconfessed sin we will not enjoy His fellowship. His presence will convict us and make us very uncomfortable until we confess and repent.

We cannot allow the standards of the world to guide our moral decisions and expect to enjoy the presence of God in our daily life.

God's standards have to do with the heart, the mind and the will as we relate to Him and others. When we walk with the Lord, in the light of His word, there is joy and contentment.

November 2

Eternity

He has made everything beautiful in its time. He has
also set eternity in the hearts of men; yet they cannot
fathom what God has done from beginning to end.
Ecclesiastes 3:11

God has "set eternity in the hearts of men." This means that we can never be completely satisfied with earthly pleasures and pursuits. Because we are created in God's image (1) we have a spiritual thirst, (2) we have eternal values, and (3) nothing but the eternal God can truly satisfy us. He has built in us a restless yearning for the kind of perfect world that can only be found in His perfect rule.

He has given us a glimpse of the perfection of His creation. But it's only a glimpse; we cannot see into the future or comprehend everything. We must trust Him. When we have the proper view of God, we discover that real pleasure is found in enjoying whatever we have as gifts from God, not as things we have accumulated.

What is the real purpose of life? It is that we should know God and worship Him in Spirit and in Truth. We experience this through Christ who is the Way to God, the Truth about God and the Life from God.

November 3

Crucified

May I never boast except in the cross of our Lord Jesus
Christ, through which the world has been crucified to
me and I to the world.

Galatians 6:14

The world is full of enticements and its sinful influence
is a temptation every day. The only way we can escape
these destructive influences is to allow the indwelling
Holy Spirit to enable us to crucify our interest in them.
It's not just a matter of what we should or shouldn't
do but it concerns the inward condition of the heart.
What matters to God is that we be completely changed
from the inside out. A transformation of our attitudes
and actions must happen. (Galatians 2:20)

How have I been crucified with Christ? I have accepted
Christ as my substitute in death. He paid the penalty
for my sin. I am no longer condemned. I am in Christ
and Christ is in me—His life is my life. He enables me
to overcome the world, the flesh, and the devil, daily,
as I yield to the power of His Spirit in me. I am being
conformed to His image.

November 4

God's Will

Therefore, I urge you brothers, in view of God's mercy, to offer your bodies as living sacrifices, holy and pleasing to God—this is your spiritual act of worship. Do not conform any longer to the patterns of this world but be transformed by the renewing of your mind. Then you will be able to test and approve what God's will is—His good, pleasing and perfect will.

Romans 12:1-2

God has good, pleasing and perfect plans for His children. He wants us to be transformed with renewed minds, living to honor and obey Him. Our refusal to conform to this world's ways must go deeper than behavior and customs—it must be firmly planted in our minds. Only when the Holy Spirit renews, reeducates, and redirects our mind are we truly transformed. (Romans 8:5)

Set your mind on things above, not on earthly things. (Colossians 3:2) This means concentrating on the eternal rather than the temporal, looking at life from God's perspective and to seek what He desires. The more we regard the world around us, as God does, the more we will live in harmony with Him.

November 5

Salvation

But God demonstrates his own love for us in this: while we were still sinners, Christ died for us. For if, when we were God's enemies, we were reconciled to him through the death of his Son, how much more, having been reconciled, shall we be saved through his life. Romans 5:8, 10

When I share my testimony concerning my salvation, I must remember that it was God's work from the beginning and continues to be His work until the end. Jesus died for my sins and He was raised to life for my justification. By His death I have been saved from the wrath of God and by His life I am being saved for the glory of God.

I was not aware of my need of a Savior until the Holy Spirit convicted me of my sinful condition. When I realized that I was helpless before a Holy God, the Holy Spirit revealed the Lord Jesus Christ to me as Savior—the one who took my place in death to pay the penalty for my sin. It was by God's grace that I was able to believe (exercise faith) in what the Holy Spirit revealed to me.

When I use phrases such as, "when I accepted Christ," "when I was saved," or, "when I asked Jesus into my heart," I need to make it clear that God made the first move to draw me unto Himself. When I turned to Him He has continued His work in me, to conform me to the image of Christ, which will bring glory to Him.

November 6

Life

Before I formed you in the womb I knew you, before you were born I set you apart; I appointed you as a prophet to the nations.
Jeremiah 1:5

God is all-seeing, all-knowing, all-powerful, and everywhere present. God knows us. (Psalm 139)

He knew me long before I was born. He thought about me and planned for me. He has a purpose in mind for me. That purpose involves loving Him, obeying Him and serving Him. At times He may have something special for me through which He will use me in a specific way. I may feel inadequate, but if He calls me He will provide all I need to fulfill His plan. The way may be rough but He will be with me through it.

I must focus on the Creator, not on creation. Victory isn't about my abilities, my strength, my skills; it has to do with His presence.

November 7

Guilt

Therefore, there is now no condemnation for those who are in Christ Jesus, because through Christ Jesus the law of the Spirit of life set me free from the law of sin and death.

Romans 8:1-2

The Spirit of Life is the Holy Spirit. He is the power behind the rebirth of every Christian. He gives us the power to live the Christian life.

When my behavior is in conflict with the Spirit of God in me I feel an emotional response, an emotional pain. That is guilt for doing wrong. Whether an action, thought, careless word or something else. Christ has already removed the burden of guilt and paid the debt for my sin, but I must take responsibility for my actions through confession and repentance. (I John 1:9)

I can better understand God's love for me when I consider my love for my children. My desire for them, when they did something wrong, was to come to me so I could discipline in love and forgiveness. It grieved my heart if they drew back in fear because of guilt.

God's love is greater far!

November 8

Storms

I will instruct you and teach you in the way you should
go; I will counsel you and watch over you.
Psalm 32:8 NIV

God allows storms in our lives for different reasons—
not always because we're out of His will. He may use
them for testing, teaching or training but His desire is
always for our good, and He works to accomplish that
end.

I need to seek discernment in the storms of my life.
Difficulties create strong emotions that cloud our
ability to think. That's why we need to turn to the
Lord for He has committed Himself to instructing us.
When we wait on Him He will give us insight into our
situation.

What He tells us may not be what we want to hear but
it will be what is best for us.

November 9

My God

Do you not know? Have you not heard? The Lord is the everlasting God, the creator of the ends of the earth. He will not grow tired or weary, and his understanding no one can fathom.

Isaiah 40:28

Isaiah describes God's power to create, His provision to sustain and His presence to help. God is almighty and all-powerful; but even so He cares for each of us personally. No person or thing can be compared to God (v. 25). We describe God as best we can with our limited knowledge and language, but we only limit our understanding of Him and His power when we compare Him to what we experience on earth.

My feelings have nothing to do with God's sovereignty. God is in control, always has been and always will be. What he says is true whether I believe it or not, I can choose to live by faith in the facts or by fear of my feelings.

November 10

Seek God

Look to the Lord and his strength; seek his face always.
Psalm 105:4

Hunger for the Lord is an acquired taste. The more we pursue Him, the greater our hunger will be. If we ignore Him we will lose what little appetite we have. Ask the Lord to put His desires in your heart and His thoughts in your mind.

Begin with the Scripture and prayer. Read and mediate on His Word—digest what you read—talk to the Lord and listen for His voice. The deep things of God don't just fall into your brain; they are placed there through diligent study.

The Christian life is meant to be a pursuit of God. To stand still after salvation is to miss the treasures that are available in Christ.

November 11

God's Word

Do not let this Book of the Law depart from your mouth;
meditate on it day and night, so that you may be careful to do
everything in it   Then you will be prosperous and successful.
Joshua 1:9

God's instruction to Joshua is also His instruction to us today. We can become so overwhelmed with all of the activity in our lives that we forget our first priority—our relationship with God—and our dependence upon Him.

Meditation is a discipline. It doesn't just happen. It involves prayerfully reading Scripture, being quiet before the Lord so He can speak to our heart, applying His truth to our lives.

As we meditate upon His Word we are hiding it in our heart and becoming more aware of His presence.

His presence is His greatest present to us!

November 12

Holiness

You shall be holy for I am holy.
I Peter 1:16

What an overwhelming command! But that is what the Lord is committed to do in our lives—make us holy. Holiness means being totally devoted and dedicated to God, set aside for His use and set apart from the influence of sin. We cannot become holy on our own but God gives us His Holy Spirit to help us overcome sin.

The Father has predestined us to be conformed to the image of His Son, and He is continually working in our lives to fulfill His purpose. (Romans 8:28-29)

If we don't cooperate with Him, the world will squeeze us into its mold and we will miss the plans He has for us. (Romans 12:1-2)

God's will for us is not that we be happy but that we be holy. We cannot become holy in a hurry. We must wait on the Lord!

November 13

God's Word

*He read it aloud from daybreak till noon ---and all the
people listened attentively to the Book of the Law.*
(God's Word) Nehemiah 8:3

Sometimes we become dull of hearing, because hearing
is a choice. The length of a person's attention span
is directly related to the intensity of his hunger for
something. If our desire is to know more of God, then
our attention will be focused on the reading of His
Word in private or public.

Nothing in the world matters as much as what the Lord
has to say. He is worthy of our undivided attention.
We should listen carefully when His Word is read and
ask the Holy Spirit to help us understand "how it
applies to our life?"

When we listen with an open heart and an alert mind
we will receive from Him.

November 14

Listening to God

Speak, Lord, for your servant is listening.
I Samuel 3:9

Whether we are studying God's Word individually or with others, our motive should be to learn more about God and His ways and to determine in our heart to obey what we hear. (Psalm 119:33) We should expect the Lord to speak specifically to us. (Psalm 25:4-5) God uses sermons, Sunday School lessons and quiet times alone to build us up, strengthen us and direct us.

As we approach God's Word our prayer should be, "Speak, Lord, for your servant is listening." Then believe and wait.

The omniscient Sovereign of the universe acts on behalf of those who wait for Him. (Isaiah 64:4)

November 15

Spiritual Understanding

We have not received the spirit of the world but the Spirit who is from God, that we may understand what God has freely given us.

I Corinthians 2:12

"I just don't understand the Bible." How often do you hear that comment? We expect to hear this from unbelievers but to hear it from one who has been a Christian for years will cause us to question, "Why?"

Some people think you have to go to college or seminary to understand the Scriptures so they depend on sermons for Bible knowledge. They spend very little time in God's Word.

The key is not education but obedience. As we act on what we read or hear, God's Word comes "alive" in our heart and we begin to understand that it is His voice to us personally. (Psalm 111:10)

The Holy Spirit, who indwells the believer, is our Teacher. (John 16:13)

November 16

Encouragement

Therefore encourage one another and build each other
up, just as in fact you are doing.
I Thessalonians 5:11

Each one of us has potential stored up inside just waiting to be developed. We are filled with promise and possibility. But for many of us, that potential is locked away behind a closed door. It may be a door of disappointment, failure, embarrassment, or lack of confidence.

Each person in your life has such doors and you hold the key to unlocking some of those doors with your words of encouragement. When we offer the gift of encouragement we have the privilege of taking part in the building up of the special people in our lives. What an opportunity to have a lasting influence.

Sometimes all it takes is one simple act of believing in someone to unlock his or her potential.

Our Hope

So this is what the Sovereign Lord says: See, I lay a stone in Zion, a tested stone, a precious cornerstone for a sure foundation; the one who trusts will never be dismayed.
Isaiah 28:16

This "cornerstone" is the Lord Jesus Christ, the foundation on whom we build our lives.

No matter how much life changes, we can have hope, for we are anchored to a firm foundation that will never be shaken.

"The Security of Our Triune God"

Our heavenly Father knows each of us by name.
(Isaiah 43:1)

Our Savior keeps every divine promise. (II Corinthians 1:20)

The Holy Spirit assures us that we are secure in Christ, both in this life and the life to come.
(Ephesians 1:13-14)

November 18

Blessings

*May God be gracious to us and bless us and make his
face shine upon us, that your ways may be known on
earth, your salvation among all nations.*
Psalm 67:1-2

This Psalm speaks of the fulfillment of the Great
Commission (Matthew 28:1-20), when Jesus
commanded that the gospel be taken to all nations.

Knowing God involves more than just having
information about God. We also need to know how
God has operated in human history, what His desire is
for us now, and what His plans are for the future.

It is God's nature to bless. His ultimate goal is far
more than just to make us happy, peaceful protected
and prosperous. He wants them to flow out to others
as part of His plan for the whole earth.

When the Lord blesses me He's not only doing
something for me; He's also doing something in and
through me to affect other lives.

November 19

Humility

Humble yourselves before the Lord and he will lift you up.
James 4:10

Man-made religions focus on human effort. Christianity focuses on Christ's work. Our salvation does not depend on our own discipline and rule keeping, but on the power of Christ's death and resurrection.

True humility means seeing ourselves as we really are from God's perspective, and acting accordingly. We practice false humility when we talk negatively about ourselves so that others will think we're spiritual. False humility is self-centered; true humility is God-centered.

A Look at Ourselves

"I dreamed death came the other night and heaven's gates swung wide;

With kindly grace an angel ushered me inside.

And there to my astonishment stood folks I'd known on earth -

Some I'd judged as "unfit" or of 'little worth.'

Indignant words rose to my lips but never were set free---

For every face showed stunned surprise---

No one expected me!"

Author Unknown

November 20

Wisdom

Get wisdom, get understanding. Wisdom is supreme;
therefore get wisdom.
Proverbs 4"5a, 7a

This is a daily process made possible through reading God's Word and prayer. (James 1:5)

It produces effective living.

It begins with reverence and respect for Almighty God.

It requires moral and practical application of God's Word, by the Holy Spirit, as I seek His leading and practice His presence. When I respond in obedience— being selective in what I see, what I hear and what I read—God will plant His truth in my heart and it will produce godly wisdom.

Prayer

Pray continually; give thanks in all circumstances.
I Thessalonians 5:17-18

My private prayer life can transform my natural human power into supernatural power. Prayer: Beholding God's Glory.

All that true prayer seeks is God Himself, for with Him we get all we need. Prayer is simply "turning the soul to God."

The highest result of prayer is not deliverance from evil or the securing of some coveted thing, but knowledge of God.

Three phases of the Christian's Prayer Life:

1) The spirit of need petition, "Lord, give me."
2) The spirit of surrender—His will, "Lord, make me."
3) The spirit of gratitude—praise, "Lord, thank you."

Requirements for answered prayer:

Acknowledge God and His power.
Recognize Jesus and the power of His name.
Believe God's Word—act in faith.

The distance from where I am to where the Lord wants to take me is measured by my willingness to pray.

November 22

God's Call

The one who calls you is faithful and he will do it.
I Thessalonians 5:24

Lack of obedience indicates a lack of trust. My worth comes from being a child of God and my value is based on what God does—not because of what I do.

My calling as an intercessor is not based on what I want God to do but on what God wants to do in answer to my praying. I am to pray in obedience and leave the answer to Him.

As God's intercessor I am a priest to other believers. (I Peter 2:9) My most powerful resource is communion with God through prayer. His desire is that I trust Him with all my heart and acknowledge Him in all my ways and He will direct my path. (Proverbs 3:5-6)

I am to trust, submit, pray and obey. Trust and submit is an attitude—pray and obey is an action.

Love

Love the Lord your God with all your heart and with all your soul and with all your mind and with all your strength. The second is this: Love your neighbor as yourself. There is no commandment greater than these.

Mark 12:30-31

Jesus said, "There is no commandment greater than, 'to love God with your total being and love your neighbor as yourself.'"

The Old Testament Law was based on these two commandments but had been extended, by the Scribes and Pharisees, to include hundreds of "do's and don'ts."

The Ten Commandments that God gave Moses could be summed up in these two—the first four, Love God. The last six—Love your neighbor.

Christ in me makes it possible for me to fulfill the Law. Through His grace I am able to love God with my total being and to love my neighbor as myself.

My greatest hindrance is majoring on the "don'ts" rather than the "do's." I need to seek positive ways to express my love.

November 24

God's Love

A new command I give you: Love one another, as I have loved you, so you must also love one another. By this all men will know that you are my disciples, if you love one another.
John 13:34-35

To love one another was not a new commandment, but to love as Jesus loves us was a new way of expressing that love. No "conditions" were attached to the "love of Jesus." He is our example. Love is more than an emotional feeling—it is an attitude that reveals itself in action. Such as:

Helping when it's not convenient, giving when it hurts, forgiving and forgetting and accepting others unconditionally.

Expressions of God's love:

Touch—through the hands and arms of others.

Time - fellowship and communion in prayer.

Encouragement—through His Word and other believers.

November 25

Learning to Wait

May integrity and uprightness protect me, because my hope is in you.
Psalm 25:21

Uprightness makes us learn God's requirements and strive to fulfill them.

Integrity - being what we say we are—keeps us from claiming to be upright while living as if we do not know God.

God not only sees us here and now but He views the big picture at once—where we've been, where we are and where we're going. He knows how every decision, action or blessing will impact our lives. What we may think is a blessing now could wreck our life later. He may withhold an answer to prayer until we're ready for the blessing. It doesn't mean He didn't hear; it means He's looking out for us.

November 26

Christian Living

Do not love the world or anything in the world. If anyone loves the world, the love of the Father is not in him.
I John 2:15 NIV

Worldliness is not limited to external behavior; the people we associate with, the places we go, or the activities we enjoy.

Worldliness is also internal because it begins in the heart. It has to do with attitudes.

> (1) The cravings of sinful man—gratifying physical desires.

> (2) The lust of the eyes—accumulating things, materialism.

> (3) Boasting of what one has and does—one's position

God values self-control, a spirit of generosity, and a commitment to humble service. It is possible to give an impression of avoiding worldly pleasures while still having worldly attitudes in the heart.

It is also possible, like Jesus, to love sinners and spend time with them while maintaining a commitment to God's kingdom.

November 27

Love

*You shall love the Lord your God with all your heart,
and with all your soul, and with all your mind, --- you
shall love your neighbor as yourself.*
Matthew 22:37, 39

Jesus said that we are to love the Lord our God with
our entire being, not just by words but by attitudes,
actions and motives. He didn't stop there but went on
to say we are to love our neighbor as ourselves. That's
a big order because we focus on ourselves most of the
time. We want what is best for ourselves.

Human nature is selfish and there is no way we can live
up to this obligation but the Lord has provided a way
for the Christian to do the impossible. The indwelling
Holy Spirit works to produce His fruit in us and first on
the list is love. (Galatians 5:22) Love can express itself
in many ways when we allow the Holy Spirit freedom
to do His work, for it is God's doing, not ours.

November 28

Life

Why, you don't even know what will happen tomorrow.
What is your life? You are a mist that appears for a little
while and then vanishes.
James 4:14

Life is short no matter how many years we live. Don't be deceived, thinking you have many years ahead to live for Christ, to enjoy life and family or to do what you know you should.

Live each day in view of eternity, choosing priorities according to God's principles. Be aware of opportunities to share the love of Christ with others. If may be only a kind word or a smile but God can use it in a special way to accomplish His will in our life and the life of someone else.

Sin

*Anyone, then, who knows the good he ought to do and
doesn't do it, sins.*
James 4:17

We usually think of sin as doing something wrong,
obvious things that others recognize in our actions.
James tells us that sin is also not doing right. These
sins are described as sins of commission and sins of
omission.

It is a sin to lie but it is also a sin to know the truth and
not tell it. It is a sin to speak evil about someone but
it is also a sin to ignore someone who needs your help
and friendship.

The same principle is true when we sense God's leading
but do not follow. We are ignoring Him and it grieves
His heart.

The person who sins a little now and then soon finds
that he sins more now than he did then.

You can't put your sins behind you until you're willing
to face them.

November 30

God's Word

*My son, do not forget my teaching, but keep my
commands in your heart, for they will prolong your life
many years and bring you prosperity.*
Proverbs 3:1-2

The Bible is the most remarkable book ever written. It
is a personal "love letter" to us from the Father. It has
often been referred to as a compass to point us in the
right direction and a map to guide us in life's journey.

God, as our Creator, knows what is best for us and He
can bring it to pass because He is Sovereign over His
Creation. We get so busy walking through life that
we forget to check God's compass to make sure we are
headed in the right direction.

As we seek God in prayer, use the Bible as our guide
and then follow His leading, He will make our paths
straight. (V. 6)

December

December 1

Discipline

My son, do not despise the Lord's discipline and do not resent his rebuke, because the Lord disciplines those he loves, as a father the son he delights in.

Proverbs 3:11-12

Discipline means to "teach and train," in love, for the best development of a person. As parents we sometimes have a problem in distinguishing between discipline and punishment. This problem may become evident in our relationship with God.

God, being the source of love, knows that in order to become morally strong and good, we must learn the difference between right and wrong. Our all-wise God knows how to administer discipline to get our individual attention. Our response should be, "I hear you Lord."

December 2

Priorities—Principles

Honor the Lord with your wealth, with the first fruits
of all your crops; then your barns will be filled to
overflowing and your vats will brim over with new wine.
Proverbs 3:9-10

God's Word is filled with His principles—guidelines to direct us in His ways. When we face decisions in life sometimes we consider the good way, or maybe a better way, and then there is the best way. God's way is always the best way.

The "first fruits' refer to the practice of giving to God's use the first and best portion of the harvest. We are often tempted to give God the "leftovers." We may be sincere and give willingly but our attitude is backward.

God is the owner of our resources. We are His managers. He deserves our best. He gave us His best.

December 3

Patience

They that wait upon the Lord shall renew their strength;
they shall mount up with wings as eagles; they shall run
and not be weary; and they shall walk and not faint.
Isaiah 40:31

Waiting is not a virtue of our human nature. It goes
against our mind, our emotions and our will. Living
in an "instant" society has had its affect on our lives in
every area.

Patience is a supernatural characteristic experienced
as the Holy Spirit produces His fruit in the believer.
If I wait upon the Lord I will be strengthened in faith.

At first glance the three verbs used to describe the
person of faith seem to be in reverse order (fly, run,
walk.) There is no form of exhaustion mentioned in
connection with those who "mount up with wings."
They that run will not be "weary," but the most
remarkable effect of all is connected with walking.
"They shall not faint."

Day to day walking with the Lord requires His strength
at work in and through us.

December 4

The Church

*Simon Peter answered, You are the Christ, the Son of
the living God. Jesus replied," --- and I tell you that you
are Peter, and on this rock I will build my church, and
the gates of Hades will not overcome it.*
Matthew 16:16, 18 NIV

There has been disagreement as to the "rock" that
Jesus was referring to. The word "Peter" means "rock"
and Jesus said to Peter, "You are a rock."

A vital principle of Scripture interpretation is "let
scripture interpret scripture."

I believe Peter does this in I Peter 2:4-8, as he describes
the Church. Christ is the living Stone, the cornerstone,
the capstone. He is the foundation on which He has
built His Church. We as individual members are living
stones being built into a spiritual house to be a holy
priesthood, offering spiritual sacrifices acceptable to
God through Jesus Christ.

Though rejected by some, Christ is the most important
part of the Church. He is the Head of the Body.

December 5

A Portrait of God

Praise the Lord, O my soul.
O Lord my God, you are very great; you are clothed with
splendor and majesty.
Psalm 104:1 NIV

God has revealed Himself in special ways through the book of Psalms. When He first made me aware that I did not know Him, as He is—God Almighty - He directed me to the Psalms. As I read and prayed through the Psalms I became more aware of the character and nature of the awesome God we worship,

Psalm 104 describes God as Creator and gives us a greater appreciation for His creative power recorded in Genesis, Chapter One. He is sovereign over His creation which He uses to accomplish His will and purpose.

God's act of creation deserves the praise of all people. Many people think they don't need God but our every breath depends on the spirit He has breathed into us. Not only do we depend on God for our life, but He also wants the best for us.

December 6

God's Love

The Lord is compassionate and gracious, slow to anger,
abounding in love.
Psalm 103:8

God is love! (I John 4:8) Our natural minds cannot fathom the depth of God's love. The world thinks that love is what makes a person feel good. The love of God has nothing to do with feelings. His love is unconditional—no reservations.

The blessings of life we enjoy each day are an expression of God's great love. No matter how difficult life's journey seems, you can always count your blessings—past, present and future. We are fragile but God's care is eternal. "For as high as the heavens are above the earth, so great is his love for those who fear (revere) him." (v. 11)

Everything everywhere is to praise the Lord. Praising God means remembering all He has done for us (v. 2) and obeying His commands (v. 18).

December 7

God Calls

If you love me you will obey what I command.
John 14:15

The call of God is not to any particular service. God's call is to Himself. He gets me into a relationship with Himself whereby I understand His call, then I do things out of love for Him.

God's call three-fold: I have been called—

1)   To believe in Jesus, Acts 16:31
2)   To abide in Jesus, John 15:4
3)   To follow Jesus, Matthew 4:19

When I believe I am saved, when I abide I bear fruit, when I follow I become like Jesus.

Without the Holy Spirit's presence, which I received when I believed in Jesus, I cannot abide in Christ.

Without abiding in Christ I cannot know Him well enough to follow Him.

If I choose not to follow Christ I will miss out on the joy and contentment God has planned for me.

December 8

Temptation

*No temptation has seized you except what is common to man.
And God is faithful; he will not let you be tempted beyond
what you can bear. But when you are tempted, he will also
provide a way out so that you can stand up under it.*

I Corinthians 10:13

There is a difference between temptation and sin.
Temptation involves a process through which our
hearts, minds and bodies are preparing for the act
of sin. We can interrupt the process and stop the
temptation. It begins with a glance. The enticement
enters our mind and we make a choice: am I going to
continue with this desire or not?

Thoughts tumble through our mind, we fantasize and
develop a desire for the object. Then come decision and
pursuit which ends in the sinful act.

Ask God to help you understand the process so you can
recognize the temptation and reject it.

December 9

Jesus Christ

But what about you? he asked. Who do you say I am?

Simon Peter answered, "You are the Christ, the Son of the living God." Matthew 16:15-16

While Jesus was on earth there were many ideas concerning who He was. He questioned His disciples as to whom they thought He was. Peter quickly responded and Jesus let him know that the Father had revealed this truth to him.

Today, we have God's Word about who Jesus is but there is still much disagreement and doubt about Him.

Our eternal destiny depends upon what we believe about Jesus Christ.

> Jesus, you're my Light and my Salvation;
> Son of God and Son of Man.
> The Rock of Ages, steadfast and sure,
> The Word of Truth on which I stand.
> You're the Way to Life Eternal,
> Always present day by day.
> You're the Hope that gives life meaning;
> The Joy and Strength along the way.
> You are Love that knows no limit;
> Never changing, always the same.
> You're the living expression of God Almighty;
> Sinless perfection, true to His Name.

December 10

Heart Talk

May the words of my mouth and the meditations of my heart be pleasing in your sight, O Lord, my Rock and my Redeemer.

Psalm 19:14

The thoughts I speak come through my mind but they originate in my heart. I must keep my heart clean so that my mind will think about what is true, pure, lovely, right and noble. (Philippians 4:8) Only then will I speak words that encourage and build up others, rather than criticize and destroy.

Lord, thank you for moments of quietness when I can meditate upon you and your Word. I don't know what you have for me today but I know that your grace is sufficient to see me through whatever I will experience, so I wait upon you.

December 11

Peace and Joy

Therefore, since we have been justified through faith,
we have peace with God through our Lord Jesus Christ,
through whom we have gained access by faith into this
grace in which we stand. Romans 5:1-2

When you see a painting of Christ on the cross what do you think about? Most of us think about the physical and emotional suffering He endured. What we fail to comprehend is the sense of being alone, separated from the Father (the cup He prayed about in the Garden.)

God is the source of our being—in Him we live and move and have our being—we're totally dependent on Him. Apart from Him we can do nothing.

During the crucifixion, far more was happening than the eye could see. In carrying out His plan of redemption, the Father turned His back on Jesus, pouring out His complete wrath on His Beloved Son, who became sin—complete sin—and died alone to pay the penalty for sin. A holy God cannot look upon sin. Never before had Jesus been separated from his Father.

Because of what Jesus experienced and my faith in Him I can enjoy God's eternal presence.

December 12

Faith

By faith he left Egypt, not fearing the king's anger; he persevered because he saw him who is invisible.
Hebrews 11:27

"For he endured, as seeing him who is unseen." (NASB) This was Moses' approach to life. He practiced the presence of God. He was confident in the Lord's power to guide, protect and overcome every obstacle.

The life of Moses, as recorded in God's Word, is one of the most interesting of any Bible character. In the eleventh chapter of Hebrews, known as the "Hall of Faith," we find this one little phrase that describes the character of Moses, in a special way. He recognized God at work in his life and he exercised faith in his promises. As a result God used him in an amazing way.

God is still the only certainty in this life. He is faithful (II Timothy 2:13), just (Psalm 89:14), and loving.

December 13

Faith

What does the Scripture say? Abraham believed God,
and it was counted to him as righteousness.
Romans 4:3 NIV

Abraham's life displayed faith in action. In the Old Testament, personal relationship with God showed itself in separation and this is symbolized in the life of Abraham by his separation from country and family.

Today, the separation is more of a mental and moral separation from the ways of the world. Faith never knows where it is being led, but it knows and loves the one who is leading. The root of faith is the knowledge of a person.

The life of faith is not a matter of mounting up with wings but a life of walking and not fainting. Abraham is a type of the life of faith because, "Abraham believed God."

December 14

A Follower

*So they pulled their boats upon shore, left everything
and followed him.*
Luke 5:11

Am I only a believer in Jesus or am I also a "follower" of Jesus?

A believer is one who has placed his trust in Jesus for salvation and has received the gift of eternal life. A follower goes beyond that, seeking to know God and obey Him. Joy comes from a consistent walk with Christ.

There are times when there is no illumination and no thrill, but just daily routine, the common task. Routine is God's way of saving us between our times of inspiration.

Obeying begins with a small step that may seem insignificant and yet that is where God wants to begin. Peter had been with Jesus and saw His mighty miracles but he always went back to his fishing. His experience this time was different. Jesus asked to use his boat, to be a part of his daily life. Peter obeyed Jesus, reluctantly, but then he realized that Jesus is concerned about our daily routine.

Obedience allows God to demonstrate His power in and through us.

December 15

Patience

Rest in the Lord and wait patiently for him.
Psalm 37:7 NASB

And so after waiting patiently, Abraham received what
was promised.
Hebrews 6:15 NIV

We live in a generation that expects instant results. Everyone struggles with some degree of impatience. We're born with this trait—it's very evident in newborn babies and can become a major characteristic throughout life, if not controlled.

The biblical definition of patience can mean both long-suffering and perseverance or not giving up under pressure. It can mean not giving God deadlines, accepting His timetable.

Patience is a fruit of the Spirit—a by-product of Christ's control. The result is inner peace and lack of stress.

The danger of impatience is that we might miss the Lord's perfect plan and His blessing.

December 16

Faith

For in the gospel a righteousness from God is revealed, a righteousness that is by faith from first to last, just as it is written; The righteous will live by faith.
Romans 1:17

Faith is a word with many meanings. It can mean faithfulness or absolute trust. It can mean confident hope—"Now faith is being sure of what we hope for and certain of what we do not see." (Hebrews 11:1)

It is important that we understand faith as Paul used the word, because he ties faith so closely to salvation. Faith is not something we do to earn salvation. It is God's grace, not our faith that saves us. Faith is a gift God gives us because He is saving us. (Ephesians 2:8)

Through the faith He gives us, He carries us from death into life. (John 5:24) We can never come to God through our own faith. Instead, we must accept His grace and allow Him to plant the seed of faith within us. With each step of faith we take, His faith in us increases.

December 17

Sanctification

May God Himself, the God of peace, sanctify you through and through. May your whole spirit, soul and body be kept blameless at the coming of our Lord Jesus Christ. The one who calls you is faithful and He will do it. I Thessalonians 5:23-24

We have been created spirit, soul and body.

Spirit—relate to God—His breath in us.

Soul—mind, emotions and will—personality.

Body—vehicle of the spirit and soul—dwelling place (temple).

When we trust Christ as our Savior, the Holy Spirit takes up residence within us. That's the moment of salvation, when we become a new creation. Yet as long as we live in our earthly bodies there will continue to be war between the old and new self.

The spirit, soul and body refer not so much to the distinct parts of a person as to the entire being of a person. This is Paul's way of saying that God must be involved in every aspect of our lives. Christ must control all of us, not just our "religious life."

December 18

Faith

Have faith in God, Jesus answered. I tell you the truth,
if anyone says to this mountain, Go throw yourself in
the sea, and does not doubt in his heart but believes that
what he says will happen, it will be done for him.

Mark 11:22-23

It has been observed that the believer experiences three levels of faith:

Little Faith

> Struggling to believe God. We hope He'll answer our prayer but we're just not sure. Our problem may be that we don't know what God has said in His Word so we have nothing to base our faith on.

Great Faith

> Seeking to believe God more and more. Allowing God's Word to shape our thinking and petitions, we can know that He will grant our request because we learn His will and ways.

Perfect Faith

> Resting in the confidence that the Lord has already accomplished what we asked because His will is our desire. We thank Him and watch His promises become a reality.

December 19

My Father

Do not fear, for I have redeemed you; I have called you
by name; you are mine!
Isaiah 43:1 NASB

Lord, I will praise you in the morning
As the dawn begins the day.
I remember all your mercies,
Your kind and loving way.
How you bless me with your presence,
All sufficient is your grace;
And the joy that fills my soul,
Knowing one day I'll see your face.
Thank you that you know me,
You have called me by my name.
You love me unconditionally,
Your faithfulness I can claim.
I rest in you, my Hope, my Peace -
For life with you shall never cease.

December 20

The Potter

*Yet, O Lord, you are our Father. We are the clay, you
are the potter; we are all the work of your hand.*

Isaiah 64:8

*Does not the potter have the right to make out of the
same lump of clay some pottery for noble purposes and
some for common use?*

Romans 9:21

The Potters Hand

As a lump of clay in the Potter's hand,
Waiting patiently to know the Master's plan -
I was useless and ugly to the world around,
As I lay unnoticed, a part of the ground.
Then a hand so gentle reaches down,
It picks me up then turns me around.
The Master Potter with His divine touch,
Presses me down and smoothes me much;
Removing all that should not be,
Until a beautiful vessel He's pleased to see.

But we have this treasure (God's Spirit) in jars of clay
to show that this all-surpassing power is from God and
not from us. II Corinthians 4:7

December 21

Trials

*Consider it pure joy, my brothers, whenever you face
trials of many kinds, because you know that the testing
of your faith develops perseverance.*
James 1:2-3

I have to confess that I consider pure joy as being a
time when everything is going well, no problems, life is
good. But James sees joy from a different perspective.
His thinking has to do with intimacy with God—getting
to know Him.

I can never know God as Love until I need to be loved.
I can never know God as comforter unless I need to be
comforted.
I can never know Him as the God who heals unless I
have been sick.
I can never know God as the one who protects unless I
am in danger.
I can only know God as my strength when I become
weak.

Each of these situations can be painful but they can
also be a source of joy as I discover more deeply who
God is.

December 22

Prayer

Pray without ceasing.
I Thessalonians 5:17 KJV

No one has time to pray, we have to take time from other valuable things in order to understand how necessary prayer is.

Prayer means that we get into union with God's view of other people. Our devotion as saints is to identify ourselves with God's interest in other lives.

One of the most subtle burdens God puts on us is discernment concerning other souls. He reveals things in order that we may take the burden of these individuals before Him. The reason for intercession is not that God answers prayer but that God tells us to pray.

Most of our prayers are taken up with our concerns, our needs, and only once in a while do we pray for what He tells us to.

Prayer: I tell God what I know He knows, in order that I may get to know it as He does.

December 23

The Trinity

The grace of the Lord Jesus Christ, and the love of God,
and the fellowship of the Holy Spirit be with you all.
II Corinthians 13:14 NIV

The word Trinity is not used in the Scripture but the truth of a three-part Godhead is biblical. Our God consists of three persons: God, the Father, God, the Son and God, the Holy Spirit. Each is characterized by the same attributes—they are eternal, omniscient, omnipotent, omnipresent and immutable. However, each one has a unique function.

The Father is our Creator. In His hands rests control of the universe and every aspect of our life. The Father oversees circumstances and events so that each situation can be used for our good and His glory.

The Son is our Savior. Jesus took on flesh and blood and became fully man—while still remaining fully God—and lived among mankind on earth. He did this so He could die to pay the penalty for our sin and to reconcile man to a Holy God. Today, He sits at the right hand of the Father interceding for us.

The Holy Spirit is our Helper. He indwells every believer, from the moment of salvation. He gives us Spiritual gifts and the power to do the work God calls us to do.

The Father, Son and Holy Spirit love us and desire only the best for followers of Jesus.

December 24

It Was for Me

God made him who had no sin to be sin for us, so that in him we might become the righteousness of God.
II Corinthians 5:21

Your feet were nailed to an old rugged cross;
Your knees were bent in shame.
Your hands were tied with arms outstretched,
While angry men blasphemed Your Name.

They pierced your side as the crowd looked on,
And the thorns pressed into your head.
"Forgive them, Father for what they do;
They don't really know," you said.

Your heart was broken; your strength was gone;
They parted your garments you had worn so long.
Your lips were parched, your throat was dry.
"My God, My God, why have you forsaken me?" you cry.

Darkness came and covered the earth
While the sin of mankind you bore.
Gasping for breath, you said, "It is finished."
Satan is defeated forevermore!

December 25

God's Love

By this all men will know that you are my disciples, if you love one another.

John 13:35

In John's gospel, Chapter 17, we have recorded the prayer of Jesus before He returned to heaven. This is really "The Lord's Prayer." He was praying for all believers. In verse 11, Jesus says, "I will remain in the world no longer, but they are still in the world, and I am coming to you. Holy Father protect them by the power of your name—the name you gave me—so that they may be one as we are one."

> I never cease to be amazed at God's
> unchanging love,
> And how He makes it known to me as
> blessings from above.
> Sometimes a prayer is whispered and my
> name goes up to Him;
> My weary soul is lifted and I have peace again.
> When all around is turmoil and I feel helpless
> on my own,
> A call, a card, a friendly word lets me know
> I'm not alone.
> For every need I have, God has His special
> way;
> His grace is all sufficient, expressed through
> others every day.

December 26

Abiding in Christ

If you abide in me and my words abide in you, ask
whatever you wish, and it will be done for you.
John 15:7 NASB

Only when we abide in Christ are we able to bear fruit that will glorify God. Abiding in Christ means: (1) believing that He is God's Son and accepting Him as Lord and Savior. (2) Believing God's Word and obeying it. (3) Relating in love to other believers.

Abiding in Jesus, what joy divine;
Resting in Him, the True Vine.
He's all that I need, come sunshine or rain;
He heals my broken heart and takes away the pain.
He's the source of my strength, my comfort and peace;
His mercy, His grace and His love never cease.
I'll trust His faithfulness to take every care;
To solve each problem offered in prayer.
All glory and honor to Jesus I give;
He is worthy to be praised every day I live.

December 27

Who is Jesus

But what about you? he asked. Who do you say I am?
Peter answered, The Christ of God.
Luke 9:20 NIV

Every person will have to answer this question, either in life or death.

"Therefore God exalted him to the highest place and gave him the name that is above every name, that at the name of Jesus every knee should bow, in heaven and on earth and under the earth, and every tongue confess that Jesus Christ is Lord, to the glory of God the Father." Philippians 2:9-11

"Jesus asked, "Who do you say I am?"
You're my light and my salvation;
Son of God and Son of Man.
The Rock of Ages, steadfast and sure,
The Word of Truth on which I stand.
You're the way to Life Eternal,
Always present day by day;
You're the Hope that gives life meaning,
My Joy and Strength along the way.
You're Love that knows no limit;
Never changing, always the same.
Living, Expression of God Almighty;
Sinless Perfection, true to His Name.

December 28

Citizenship

But our citizenship is in heaven. And we eagerly await
a Savior from there, the Lord Jesus Christ.
Philippians 3:20 NIV

Focusing on Christ is not natural, neither is it easy but it can bring confidence and contentment into our life, when we are dealing with difficult situations. We may not be happy but we can be assured that God is in control, for He is Sovereign. (Psalm 103:19)

"When times are good be happy; but when times are bad, consider: God has made the one as well as the other." (Ecclesiastes 7:14a)

God allows both good times and bad times to come to everyone. He blends them in our lives in such a way that we can't predict the future or count on human wisdom and power. When life appears certain and controllable, don't get too comfortable or God may allow bad times to drive you back to Him.

I'm reminded of the old song we used to sing: "This world is not my home, I'm just a passing through."

Heaven

No eye has seen, no ear has heard, no mind has conceived
what God has prepared for those who love him.
I Corinthians 2:9

HOME AT LAST

I'm walking on streets of gold,
Watching the beauty of Heaven unfold.
Ear has not heard; eye has not seen,
What God has prepared, our mind can only dream.

The saints are rejoicing, voices lifted in praise,
To the Lamb who was slain but now is raised.
Crowns are laid before the throne of our Lord,
As we bow in adoration of Christ the Living Word.

I'm talking with loved ones and saints of old,
As we stroll by the river, what beauty to behold.
No sun, no moon, but the brightness is here,
For Jesus the Light is shining everywhere.

I'm waiting to see you when God brings you home.
Longing to welcome you where you belong.
So look for His coming as the time draws near,
For our reunion in Heaven of those we hold dear.

December 30

God's Promises

For no matter how many promises God has made, they are "yes" in Christ. And so through him the "amen" is spoken by us to the glory of God.
II Corinthians 1:20 NIV

All of God's promises of what the Messiah would be like are fulfilled in Him. Jesus was faithful in His ministry. (I Peter 3:18) He never sinned; He died for us (Hebrews 2:9); now He faithfully intercedes for us. (Romans 8:34, Hebrews 4:14-15)

God is glorified as His promises, in Christ, are fulfilled through believers as we exercise faith in Him.

Claiming God's Promises:

> Some are conditional, some unconditional
> Some a general, some specific
> Some are for present time, some for the future.
> Some to nations, some to individuals.
> Some to Jews, some to Gentiles.
> Some to Israel, some tot the Church.
> Some to believers, some to unbelievers.

May God himself, the God of peace, sanctify you through and through. May your whole spirit, soul and body be kept blameless at the coming of our Lord Jesus Christ. The one who calls you is faithful and he will do it. (I Thessalonians 5:23-24)

December 31

Grace

He was delivered over to death for our sins and was raised to life for our justification. Therefore, since we have been justified through faith, we have peace with God, through our Lord Jesus Christ, through whom we have gained access by faith into this grace in which we now stand.

Romans 4:25-5:2

We are saved by God's grace and we are also sustained by His grace. How does it work out in our everyday life?

1)   The Lord's grace releases His supernatural power within us so we can endure life's hardships and rejoice in what God is doing in and through us.

2)   Grace encourages us in our faith in His sovereignty.

3)   We are assured of His sustaining presence day by day.

4)   As we experience His care for us we are able to encourage others.

5)   During hard times grace works to transform our character so others can see Jesus reflected in us.

Too often we acknowledge our salvation is by God's grace alone but we try to live daily by our own strength.

We need a daily dose of God's grace to enable us to live a victorious Christian life.

I met God in the morning,
When my day was at its best,
And His presence came like Sunrise,
Like Glory in my breast,
So I think I know the Secret,
Learned from many a troubled way,
You must seek Him in the morning,
If you want Him through the day.

Author Unknown